SIDNEY POITIER

Carol Bergman

Senior Consulting Editor
Nathan Irvin Huggins
Director
W.E.B. Du Bois Institute for Afro-American Research
Harvard University

CHELSEA HOUSE PUBLISHERS
New York   Philadelphia

Editor-in-Chief   Nancy Toff

Executive Editor   Remmel T. Nunn

Managing Editor   Karyn Gullen Browne

Copy Chief   Juliann Barbato

Picture Editor   Adrian G. Allen

Art Director   Giannella Garrett

Manufacturing Manager   Gerald Levine

Staff for SIDNEY POITIER

Senior Editor   Richard Rennert

Associate Editor   Perry King

Assistant Editor   Gillian Bucky

Copy Editor   Ellen Scordato

Editorial Assistant   Susan DeRosa

Associate Picture Editor   Juliette Dickstein

Picture Researcher   Nisa Rauschenberg

Senior Designer   Laurie Jewell

Design Assistant   Laura Lang

Production Coordinator   Joseph Romano

Cover Illustration   Alan J. Nahigian

Creative Director   Harold Steinberg

Copyright © 1988 by Chelsea House Publishers, a division of
Main Line Book Co. All rights reserved. Printed and bound in
the United States of America.

3   5   7   9   8   6   4

Library of Congress Cataloging in Publication Data

Bergman, Carol.
    Sidney Poitier.

    (Black Americans of achievement)
    Bibliography: p.
    Includes index.
    Summary: Traces the life of the movie actor who won an
Academy Award in 1963 and became a symbol of the break-
through of black performers in motion pictures.
    1. Poitier, Sidney—Juvenile literature.   2. Actors—
United States—Biography—Juvenile literature. [1. Poitier,
Sidney.   2. Actors and actresses.   3. Afro-Americans—Bi-
ography]   I. Title.   II. Series.
PN2287.P57B47   1988   791.43′028′0924 [B] [92]   87-24250
ISBN 1-55546-605-2
    0-7910-0209-8   (pbk.)

CONTENTS

——— ◀♥▶ ———

BLACK
AMERICANS
OF
ACHIEVEMENT

---·❦·---

MUHAMMAD ALI
heavyweight champion

RICHARD ALLEN
*founder of the
African Methodist
Episcopal church*

LOUIS ARMSTRONG
musician

JAMES BALDWIN
author

BENJAMIN BANNEKER
*scientist and
mathematician*

MARY MCLEOD BETHUNE
educator

BLANCHE K. BRUCE
politician

RALPH BUNCHE
diplomat

GEORGE WASHINGTON CARVER
botanist

CHARLES WADDELL CHESTNUTT
author

PAUL CUFFE
abolitionist

FREDERICK DOUGLASS
abolitionist editor

CHARLES R. DREW
physician

W. E. B. DUBOIS
educator and author

PAUL LAURENCE DUNBAR
poet

DUKE ELLINGTON
bandleader and composer

RALPH ELLISON
author

ELLA FITZGERALD
singer

MARCUS GARVEY
black-nationalist leader

PRINCE HALL
social reformer

WILLIAM H. HASTIE
educator and politician

MATTHEW A. HENSON
explorer

CHESTER HIMES
author

BILLIE HOLIDAY
singer

JOHN HOPE
educator

LENA HORNE
entertainer

LANGSTON HUGHES
poet

JAMES WELDON JOHNSON
author

SCOTT JOPLIN
composer

MARTIN LUTHER KING, JR.
civil rights leader

JOE LOUIS
heavyweight champion

MALCOLM X
militant black leader

THURGOOD MARSHALL
Supreme Court justice

ELIJAH MUHAMMAD
religious leader

JESSE OWENS
champion athlete

GORDON PARKS
photographer

SIDNEY POITIER
actor

ADAM CLAYTON POWELL, JR.
political leader

A. PHILIP RANDOLPH
labor leader

PAUL ROBESON
singer and actor

JACKIE ROBINSON
baseball great

JOHN RUSSWURM
publisher

SOJOURNER TRUTH
antislavery activist

HARRIET TUBMAN
antislavery activist

NAT TURNER
slave revolt leader

DENMARK VESEY
slave revolt leader

MADAME C. J. WALKER
entrepreneur

BOOKER T. WASHINGTON
educator

WALTER WHITE
political activist

RICHARD WRIGHT
author

ON ACHIEVEMENT

— ❧ —

Coretta Scott King

BEFORE YOU BEGIN this book, I hope you will ask yourself what the word excellence means to you. I think that it's a question we should all ask, and keep asking as we grow older and change. Because the truest answer to it should never change. When you think of excellence, perhaps you think of success at work; or of becoming wealthy; or meeting the right person, getting married, and having a good family life.

Those important goals are worth striving for, but there is a better way to look at excellence. As Martin Luther King, Jr., said in one of his last sermons, "I want you to be first in love. I want you to be first in moral excellence. I want you to be first in generosity. If you want to be important, wonderful. If you want to be great, wonderful. But recognize that he who is greatest among you shall be your servant."

My husband, Martin Luther King, Jr., knew that the true meaning of achievement is service. When I met him, in 1952, he was already ordained as a Baptist preacher and was working towards a doctoral degree at Boston University. I was studying at the New England Conservatory and dreamed of accomplishments in music. We married a year later, and after I graduated the following year we moved to Montgomery, Alabama. We didn't know it then, but our notions of achievement were about to undergo a dramatic change.

You may have read or heard about what happened next. What began with the boycott of a local bus line grew into a national movement, and by the time he was assassinated in 1968 my husband had fashioned a black movement powerful enough to shatter forever the practice of racial segregation. What you may not have read about is where he got his method for resisting injustice without compromising his religious beliefs.

He got the strategy of nonviolence from a man of a different race, who lived in a distant country, and even practiced a different religion. The man was Mahatma Gandhi, the great leader of India, who devoted his life to serving humanity in the spirit of love and nonviolence. It was in these principles that Martin discovered his method for social reform. More than anything else, those two principles were the key to his achievements.

This book is about black Americans who served society through the excellence of their achievements. It forms a part of the rich history of black men and women in America—a history of stunning accomplishments in every field of human endeavor, from literature and art to science, industry, education, diplomacy, athletics, jurisprudence, even polar exploration.

Not all of the people in this history had the same ideals, but I think you will find something that all of them have in common. Like Martin Luther King, Jr., they all decided to become "drum majors" and serve humanity. In that principle—whether it was expressed in books, inventions, or song—they found something outside themselves to use as a goal and a guide. Something that showed them a way to serve others, instead of living only for themselves.

Reading the stories of these courageous men and women not only helps us discover the principles that we will use to guide our own lives, but it teaches us about our black heritage and about America itself. It is crucial for us to know the heroes and heroines of our history and to realize that the price we paid in our struggle for equality in America was dear. But we must also understand that we have gotten as far as we have partly because America's democratic system and ideals made it possible.

We still are struggling with racism and prejudice. But the great men and women in this series are a tribute to the spirit of our democratic ideals and the system in which they have flourished. And that makes their stories special, and worth knowing. ❧

SIDNEY POITIER

1
A LONG JOURNEY'S END

On THE NIGHT of April 14, 1964, a tense Sidney Poitier sat in the Santa Monica Civic Auditorium in Santa Monica, California, waiting for the American motion picture industry's announcement of the winner of that year's Academy Award for Best Actor. The 37-year-old actor had been nominated for the award for his starring role in *Lilies of the Field*. His portrayal of Homer Smith—the bighearted ex-soldier who builds a church for a group of German nuns in the Arizona desert—had been selected as one of the five best performances of the year.

Although Poitier had been nominated for the Best Actor award once before, he was surprised that his *Lilies of the Field* performance had earned him so much attention. Still, the possibility of winning the award seemed extremely remote to him. No black person had ever won the Academy Award for Best Actor or Best Actress.

Quiet fell on the auditorium as the actress Anne Bancroft announced the nominees for the award: Albert Finney for *Tom Jones*, Richard Harris for *This Sporting Life*, Sidney Poitier for *Lilies of the Field*, Paul Newman for *Hud*, and Rex Harrison for *Cleopatra*.

Tough competition, thought Poitier, reflecting back on his years of struggle to attain his present position in the film industry. He had come to Hollywood in 1950, at a time when movie studios, re-

Academy Award-winners Poitier and Italian film director Federico Fellini share a word after the 1964 Academy Awards ceremonies in the Santa Monica Civic Auditorium.

11

Filmed in only 14 days on an extremely small budget, Lilies of the Field *became one of the most popular movies of 1963. Poitier plays a former soldier who befriends a group of German nuns and helps them erect a chapel in the New Mexico desert.*

sponding to an increasing public awareness of racial problems in America, were just beginning to cast black actors in important, multidimensional roles. In an earlier era, he would have had no chance of starring in a Hollywood film.

From the beginnings of the movie industry in the 1890s through World War I, film studios rarely employed black actors and actresses even though there were many excellent ones in the theater and traveling vaudeville shows. Most of the roles requiring a black actor were played by white actors whose faces and hands were daubed black with burnt cork. The sight of these men and women with such makeup on their faces would have been downright hilarious if it had not been such a blatant expression of institutionalized racism.

The first black actors to appear on screen had to cover their skin with burnt cork, too. They were forced to caricature blacks in the same manner that white actors did. The characters that these actors played usually portrayed blacks in a very unflattering light.

Not surprisingly, a black film industry that was separate from the white film industry soon emerged. By the 1920s, there were more than 30 independent black film production companies serving more than 700 movie houses in black communities across America. The most famous of these companies was run by Oscar Micheaux, who produced, directed, and distributed more than 44 films from 1918 to 1948. Few

Stepin Fetchit (right) delighted audiences with his comedic antics in the 1930s. Yet his presence in movies also helped the film industry to maintain its image of blacks as second-class citizens.

whites ever saw these low-budget, sometimes hastily made films, which received little attention from the main film establishment.

In 1927, when sound was introduced into film-making—with the release of *The Jazz Singer*, featuring entertainer Al Jolson occasionally in blackface—black performers were suddenly in demand. Large numbers of blacks were brought to Hollywood to play singers, musicians, and dancers appearing in the background of many films. The standard roles for these blacks—as maids, clowns, happy slaves, devoted servants, flamboyant musicians, and athletes—did not change significantly until racial equality began to emerge as a social issue in the 1930s.

From the 1930s to the 1950s, several serious films were made that dealt with the problems of racial inequality. But these films were the exception. For the most part, black actors and actresses continued to be offered demeaning roles only. Stepin Fetchit, a bumbling clown who was to become film's first black millionaire, embodied the movie industry's image of blacks. Hattie McDaniel became the most successful and popular black actress during this era. However, even after she won the Academy Award as Best Supporting Actress for her portrayal of Scarlett O'Hara's slave in *Gone with the Wind*, she was never allowed to stray from racial typecasting. She was only offered roles as a devoted mammy or a maid.

During the 1930s and 1940s, the great black actor and singer Paul Robeson attempted to change Hollywood's conception of blacks. However, he had little success, and he consequently made most of his films in England.

Poitier's first 20 years in Hollywood, from 1950 to 1970, saw some of the most rapid changes in race relations in American history. Poitier rode the crest of this new wave. Film roles became available to him that had not been offered to previous actors. He did

Actress Hattie McDaniel (left) is presented with the Oscar for Best Supporting Actress in 1940 by actress Fay Bainter. Despite receiving acclaim for her acting in Gone with the Wind, *McDaniel was subsequently offered roles only as slaves or maids.*

"Having to persevere against un-speakable odds," Poitier said, "we are capable of infinitely more than the culture is yet willing to credit to our account."

the most professional job that he could with even the shallowest of scripts. In *Lilies of the Field*, he was fortunate to have strong material with which to work, and he gave a performance that was worthy of an Academy Award nomination.

In the auditorium at Santa Monica, Anne Ban-croft was handed the envelope containing the name of the winner of the award for Best Actor. Sweat began to appear on Poitier's forehead. He had prepared an acceptance speech in case he won, but he felt sure that he would not need it. Then he heard Bancroft say, "The winner is . . . Sidney Poitier for *Lilies of the Field*."

Poitier flew to his feet and ran to the stage. People reached out to touch him, forming an honor guard and carrying him forward with their applause. At the podium, he stood wordless, his acceptance speech gone from his head. Then he heard Bancroft whispering in his ear, "So happy . . . so happy," and he knew what he wanted to say. "It has been a long journey to this moment," he began with deep feeling as he hoisted his trophy—an Oscar—into the air.

Speaking to reporters after the ceremony, Poitier said, "I was happy for me, but I was also happy for the 'folks.' We had done it. We black people had done it."

Recalling the pictures he had seen when he was young, Poitier said, "I used to go to pictures and when I saw a Negro on the screen I always left the theater feeling embarrassment and uneasiness. There was the Negro, devoid of any dignity—good maids who laughed too loudly, good butlers afraid of ghosts. I want to make motion pictures about the dignity, nobility, the magnificence of human life."

In the years since his Academy Award triumph, Poitier has attempted to challenge the movie industry's racial taboos. He has not always been successful in these attempts, but his efforts have helped to open up many new opportunities for black actors and actresses that were not present for Hattie McDaniel, Paul Robeson, or even the young Sidney Poitier. ◖◗

2

BOYHOOD
IN THE
BAHAMAS

SIDNEY POITIER WAS born on February 20, 1927, in Miami, Florida. His parents had not intended that he be born in the United States. Evelyn and Reginald Poitier were farmers from the Bahamas, and they had come to Miami a few weeks prior to Sidney's birth to sell their crop of tomatoes at the city's produce market. Evelyn was hoping to rest and have a brief vacation away from her six children during the final months of her pregnancy. But the onset of labor pains two months before the expected delivery date changed her plans.

Only Evelyn Poitier thought that the premature, three-pound infant would survive. Shortly after the delivery, Sidney's father visited an undertaker in Miami and came back with a small casket. Evelyn ignored his pessimism. Although she had lost other babies, she was convinced that Sidney would overcome his early difficulties. Not normally a superstitious person, she went to see a fortune-teller, hoping to hear something positive about her new son's future. From the depths of a trance, the woman told her, "He will be rich and famous. Your name will be carried all over the world."

Sidney gradually grew stronger, and three months after his birth, his parents brought him to his home

Poitier was raised on lush Cat Island, one of the most beautiful of the 700 islands and cays that make up the Bahamas.

Reflecting on his idyllic early years on Cat Island, Poitier said, "There was no juvenile delinquency, no marijuana, no gang membership, no drinking, and no prostitution."

on Cat Island, a small island in the Bahamas. A chain of islands lying in the Atlantic Ocean to the east of Florida, the Bahamas were discovered by Christopher Columbus in 1492. The Bahamas had been ruled by the British since the late 18th century, and like other islands in the West Indies, their history had been marked by slavery and colonialism. The Poitiers traced their name to the West Indian nation of Haiti, which was a part of the French colonial empire until it won its independence in 1804. Reginald Poitier's slave ancestors had worked on sugar plantations in Haiti and then escaped to the Bahamas, where they had lived as free men and women. Evelyn Poitier's descendants, the Outtens, had been slaves in the Bahamas. Both families, the Outtens and the Poitiers, eventually settled on Cat Island, where they had lived modest, hardworking lives as farmers for several generations.

When the Poitiers landed at Cat Island, they were greeted by their six other surviving children, who had been cared for by relatives in their parents' absence. Sidney was to be the last of the Poitier children, the others being his brothers Cyril, Reginald, Carl, and Cedric, and his sisters Ruby and Teddy. Once on Cat Island, Sidney was immediately absorbed into a large and loving extended family that included many of the relatives of his mother and father.

In such a large family environment, there are complex relationships and allegiances. Sidney learned quickly that he was part of a unit, and that everyone in the family must look out for everyone else. In the Poitier household, children who were more than six years old were expected to help with the chores on the family's farm. Evelyn Poitier imposed a strong discipline on her children, giving them a sense of pride, responsibility, and self-reliance.

Married to Reginald Poitier when she was only 13 years old, Evelyn Poitier was only 32 years old when Sidney was born. A shy, thin woman, she walked with a limp because one of her legs was shorter than the other, and her many pregnancies and long years of physical toil left her somewhat hardened. Her youngest son has said that she had a difficult time expressing her emotions. In any case, the special feelings that she experienced for the frail, young Sidney subsided after she returned to the business of raising a large, demanding family.

When Sidney was 10 months old, his mother decided he must learn how to swim, a necessity for every island child who lives near the water. The swimming lessons consisted of throwing Sidney into the ocean while she and Reginald sat in a boat watching as the baby sputtered and screamed. When Sidney began to sink beneath the water, his father scooped him out of the water and handed him to Evelyn, who promptly threw him back into the sea. After many such dunkings, he finally learned how to swim— months before he learned how to walk. He was then allowed to do whatever he wanted until he became old enough to help with the family work. Most of his early years were spent roaming around the island.

Sidney's father was more lenient with the children, perhaps because he was older and suffered from rheumatism and arthritis. These afflictions kept him subdued, although they did not prevent him from being a perfectionist when it came to tomato farming. He planted by the cycles of the moon and planned his harvests according to weather patterns. However, the huge size of his tomatoes was due more to his liberal use of bat manure than to his planting schedules. Most of his produce was sold in the United States.

Nassau, the capital of the Bahamas, became a tropical refuge for many displaced farmers during the Great Depression. The Poitier family moved there in 1937, after the tomato market on Cat Island collapsed.

While growing up, Sidney felt closest to his 11-year-older sister Teddy, an affectionate, mischievous girl who infected him with the same spirit. He looked upon his first 10 years as an almost idyllic existence, living carefree and comfortably on an island paradise without schools or cars, where children spent the whole day outside in a usually temperate climate. The island's lush vegetation included groves of coconut palms and wild edible fruit and berries. The families on the tiny island all knew one another, and they traded goods and services among themselves. In this supportive community, no one went hungry and no family felt poor.

Sidney's secure and happy childhood was abruptly shattered in 1937, when he was 10 years old. During that year, the effects of the worldwide economic depression hit the tomato farmers of Cat Island. In order to protect the livelihood of its own struggling farmers, the United States placed an embargo on imports of fresh produce from the Bahamas and other areas. The fragile economic base of Cat Island's farmers quickly collapsed. In desperation, Sidney's father decided to move the family to Nassau, the capital city of the Bahamas, where, he reasoned, there would be work for him, Evelyn, and the older children.

Most of the poor farmers who moved to Nassau from the smaller Bahamian islands believed that the city was a place where they could improve their economic situation. Some of the Poitiers' relatives were living in Nassau, and others had moved to American cities. From a distance, they seemed to be doing fairly well. But Reginald and Evelyn Poitier were realistic, pragmatic people. They had few hopes and fewer sentimental illusions about moving their family to an urban environment. They probably would never have left Cat Island if they could have avoided it. Reginald was aging rapidly and was not well. He knew that Evelyn would have to work even harder to support the family.

Poitier first experienced the bustle of urban life as well as the crippling effects of poverty at the age of 10, when his family moved to the city of Nassau.

Sidney looked upon the move to Nassau as a great adventure. Unaware of the problems his family would face in the city, he was thrilled when his father told him he would be traveling ahead with his mother to find a house for the family. From the stories of relatives, Sidney had formed in his mind a picture of the city as "tall buildings and lights, lights." Nassau did not disappoint him, and he was impressed by its bustling population, cars, and electricity. On their first day in the city, Evelyn bought her son his first ice cream cone. He was shocked that anything could be so cold.

The novelty of city life quickly vanished as Sidney watched his parents struggle against the oppression of urban poverty. No longer having the cushion of the supportive farm community to fall back upon in times of trouble, the Poitiers found it much more difficult to make a living. Sidney's father took a variety of menial jobs, while Evelyn worked for 20 cents an hour pulverizing rock into gravel for cement. Reginald Poitier attempted to grow some vegetables on a plot of ground, but he was never able to raise enough food to feed his family.

The older children worked and brought home their meager earnings. Teddy and Ruby, both already married and with young children of their own, shared whatever they had in the same spirit of the caring, extended family in which they had been raised. Sidney was enrolled in school, but he was often absent from classes. Having previously lived a relatively solitary life on a small island, he now had the opportunity to play with many boys his own age. He was aware of his parents' difficulties and he sometimes went hungry, but his new friends distracted him from his troubles.

In Nassau, Sidney was first exposed to movies. He saw many westerns starring such cowboy film idols as Tom Mix, Bob Steele, Gene Autry, and Roy Rogers. Mesmerized by these gunslingers who seemed so real to him up on the screen, he used to go behind the stage after the movie to look for his heroes, expecting them to swagger out. When he could not find them, he decided that someday he would move to Hollywood, which he believed was the home of all cowboys. Caught up in the mannerisms of the westerns, he developed a swagger of his own, which he used to impress the local girls.

Between his sporadic attendance at school and visits to the movie theater, Poitier got into mischief with his best friend, Yorick Rolle. The boys were wild at times, and as they grew older they turned from harmless pranks to more serious trouble. When he was 13 years old, Sidney slept with a prostitute and contracted gonorrhea. Then Yorick was arrested for

Roy Rogers (shown here) was one of the many film heroes idolized by Poitier when he was a boy. Poitier's statement to his sister that he was "going to Hollywood and be a cowboy" came true years later when he starred in a western, Duel at Diablo.

stealing a bicycle and sent to a reform school. Shortly afterward, Sidney was arrested for stealing corn and spent a night in jail.

Sidney sat for hours waiting for his father to come and bail him out; while he was in jail, he began to feel what Yorick must have been experiencing in reform school. When his father arrived, he was angry and concerned. On the way home, Reginald told his son wearily, "You know boy, I can't run after you anymore." In the judge's chambers the next day, Sidney felt contrite and humiliated as his father paid for the stolen corn with borrowed money.

With Sidney seemingly on the road to more trouble, Reginald and Evelyn Poitier decided to send him to the United States, where they hoped he would have an opportunity to make something of himself. Sidney's oldest brother, Cyril, had moved to Miami many years before and had an American-born wife and a large family. He was happy to send the money for Sidney to come to the United States and provide him with a place to stay. Because Sidney had been born in Miami, he was already an American citizen.

Just before he left the Bahamas, Sidney went to visit Yorick at the reformatory. When he saw how frightened and desperate-looking his friend had become, Sidney knew that his parents had made the right decision for him. "That place Nassau," he wrote, "was not good for raising tomatoes or children." ❧

3

TROUBLED TIMES

❧

POITIER LEFT NASSAU on an old Miami-bound passenger steamship in early January 1943. Then nearly 16 years old, he had mixed feelings about leaving Nassau, the comforts of home, and his new girlfriend. But he was excited, too, and he was hopeful that America really was the land of opportunity as he had been told since he was a child.

Evelyn Poitier said good-bye to her youngest child at home. She gently pushed Poitier out the door as she began to cry. His father took him to the boat. He seemed strangely unmoved by the occasion, and Poitier could see no signs of regret on Reginald's face. At the dock, his father gave him three dollars. Saying simply, "Take care of yourself, son," he waved Poitier out into the world. The young man immediately felt very alone.

Living with his brother Cyril's family in Miami, Poitier experienced institutionalized racial discrimination for the first time. "Racism was all over the place liked barbed wire," he said later. "And I kept running into it and lacerating myself." Cyril's letters had not prepared him for the realities of the segregated South. He saw signs everywhere stating "white" and "colored," indicating which public restrooms, drinking fountains, park benches, and bus seats a

In the Deep South, Poitier was confronted with Jim Crow laws (reflected in the signs shown here) for the first time in his life.

black person could use. Poitier was puzzled by these strange restrictions. He had never faced this type of discrimination in the Bahamas, where a small group of white British colonial officials ruled over the islands' black population. There the races were separated by distinct class boundaries, and overt racism was far less evident. In the South, segregation was enforced through measures known as the Jim Crow laws, which barred blacks from certain schools, hotels, and restaurants. In addition, discriminatory laws were used to keep blacks from voting or obtaining their legal rights.

"While admittedly I was not completely naive about racial matters," Poitier said about his first months in the United States, "I was certainly not afraid of white people." However, many whites were afraid of the tall, dark-skinned teenage boy who spoke with the strange, lilting accent of a West Indian. Poitier's ignorance of the accepted social rules in the segregated South soon got him in trouble.

After he moved to Miami, Poitier took a job as a delivery boy for Burdine's department store. On one of his first days on the job, he was assigned to deliver a package to a house in the wealthy Miami Beach area. Arriving at the address, he walked up to the front door and rang the bell. A woman answered. Startled that a black youth should be standing at her front door, she told Poitier sternly to go to the back door. He did not understand the reason for this request—that the back door was to be used by servants—and he asked why he should go around to the back door when he was already at the front door. The woman slammed the door in Poitier's face, and he decided to leave the package on her steps.

Two evenings later, members of the Ku Klux Klan, a violent white supremacist group, came to Cyril's house and demanded to see Poitier. Fortunately, he was not at home, and the white-hooded men departed after making some threats. Terrified that the Klansmen would return and harm his family, Cyril asked his brother to move in with their uncle Joe, who lived a few blocks away.

Poitier's uncle and his wife were kind, elderly people from the Bahamas, and he soon felt at home with them. His small room in their house became a refuge from the hardships he was discovering outside. In February 1943, during the middle of World War II, there were many jobs available because many working men were fighting overseas. However, Poitier learned quickly that job openings for a semi-literate teenager from the West Indies were limited. He worked as a dishwasher, busboy, and car washer,

A fiery cross lights up the sky at a rally of the white supremacist organization known as the Ku Klux Klan. A visit to his home by members of the Klan prompted Poitier to flee from Miami.

Upon arriving in Miami, Florida, to live with his brother's family in 1943, Poitier experienced culture shock. He said of his first encounters with the American people, "I spoke with a different kind of accent from theirs and knew nothing of the kind of life they lived."

moving restlessly from one menial task to another. Although he had only the vaguest idea of how to drive a car, he nonetheless was able to talk his way into brief stints as a parking lot attendant. Leaving a trail of damaged cars and irate parking lot owners in his wake, he learned how to drive after only a few days.

Eventually, Poitier decided to enlist in the navy. To apply, he had to display his birth certificate, which he could only get at the Bureau of Vital Statistics in downtown Miami. As a black person, he was required to get a pass from the main police station in order to enter the Records Bureau building. Once again, Poitier seemed oblivious to the segregationist protocol of the South.

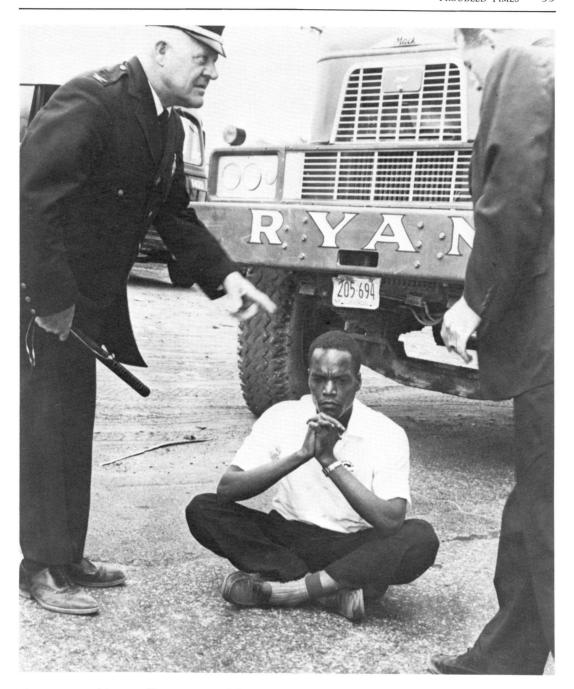

An impassioned but steadfast man peacefully registers his protest against racial injustice. In 1943, after having spent just a brief time in America, Poitier became determined to escape the racial oppression of the Deep South.

When he walked into the all-white police station, a burly desk sergeant said to him, "Take off that cap, nigger." Startled, Poitier looked around him, not being sure of to whom the man was talking. After a brief exchange with the officer, Poitier informed him that his name was not "nigger" or "boy" but rather "Sidney Poitier." Fortunately, the policemen who witnessed the incident decided to leave him alone, perhaps because they were so amused at his accent. They even gave him his pass to the Records Bureau.

Poitier received his birth certificate, only to learn that he was too young to join the navy. Unsettled by the racial situation in the South, he made plans to travel north. Afraid that his brother and uncle would not let him go, he decided to run away. He ran into trouble on his first day on the road when five officers in a police car stopped him as he was trying to hitch a ride in a "white" section of the city. As he began to answer the policemen's questions about what he was doing, he suddenly felt the nozzle of a revolver pressing against his forehead. The policemen ordered him to walk to his home without turning his head, and they followed a short distance behind him the whole way back.

Poitier was enraged by the incident, but he was also frightened enough to know that he had to leave Miami. He kept pushing northward and finally got a dishwashing job in a mountain resort in Georgia. After a few months on the job, he saved enough money to pay for a bus ticket to New York City. There he hoped to find the opportunities that were plainly unavailable for black people in the South.

Arriving in New York in the middle of 1943, Poitier realized that he was alone again, with no friends or relatives to help him. Wandering aimlessly around the city, he began to feel that New York had a strange beauty to it. He investigated the subways, the movie theaters, the hot dog stands. He visited

Poitier first arrived in New York City at the age of 16, with only a few dollars to his name. "My eyes and ears immediately began drinking in the sights and sounds swirling around me," he said.

Homeless and penniless like the man shown here, Poitier was forced to spend his first days and nights in New York on the streets of the city.

the busy streets of Harlem, the northern area of New York's Manhattan island, and he was amazed to learn that black people really lived in the tall, stately buildings he saw all around him. To the 16 year old, Harlem appeared to be his promised land.

But living in New York was expensive, and Poitier could not afford to rent a hotel room. He found a job as a dishwasher in a restaurant and then had to spend his first night sleeping in a bus station's restroom. Two days later, he moved his home to the top of a building in midtown Manhattan and slept under newspapers between his shifts at the restaurant. However, he was not disheartened, and he was soon able to save enough money to get himself a room in Harlem.

Unfortunately, Poitier was completely unprepared for the New York winter. He had no warm clothes, and the cold simply immobilized him. He lost his job and was kicked out of his room. Shortly afterward, he was arrested for vagrancy while sleeping in a train station.

The fierce New York winter took the Caribbean-born Poitier by surprise. "I was fractured, disoriented, almost immobilized," he said. "My feeble defense was to wear all of my clothes at once."

Poitier joined the United States Army in November 1943—while he was still a teenager—to take shelter from the cruel New York weather.

After being released from jail, Poitier decided to join the army so that he could be fed and clothed. He lied about his age, saying he was 18 years old, and easily passed the army's physical. Thus, in November 1943, he was accepted into the army. Private Sidney Poitier hoped that the army would send him to a base in a state with a warm climate. Instead, he was assigned to a Veteran's Administration hospital in Northport, New York, where he was trained as a medical attendant working with mentally ill patients.

At first, the tour of duty seemed ideal to Poitier. After all, he had not been sent to fight in Europe or on a Pacific island. In the army, he felt like he was part of a team, and by talking to other servicemen he learned a great deal about surviving in the city. On weekends, he went dancing at the Savoy Ballroom in New York.

However, Poitier soon became upset by the way the hospital staff treated the patients. After almost a year in the service, he decided that he wanted to get out of the army. Not willing to confess that he was underage and should never have been allowed to enlist, he decided to try for a discharge from the army on the grounds of a Section 8, which meant having himself declared mentally unfit for duty.

Accordingly, Poitier began to study for his first important acting role—as a crazy man. He threw a chair at a doctor and pushed over a cartload of dinner trays. He was quickly confined to a psychiatric ward. When the psychiatrist assigned to his case threatened to give him shock treatments, Poitier admitted that he was faking insanity to get out of the army. He could have been court-martialed and sentenced to a long prison term, but the psychiatrist took an interest in his case and recommended that he be released from the service.

Poitier became a civilian again on December 11, 1944, two months before his 18th birthday. Although he could not afford a trip to the Bahamas, he had more money in his pockets than he ever had before. He now felt more capable of dealing with the problems of living in New York City. This time he was determined to make his fortune and to find the career opportunity that had so far eluded him. ❧

4

ACTORS WANTED

WHILE POITIER WAS in the army, he had learned how to survive in the city, and his year in the service had given him some much-needed time to mature. When he returned to New York City in December 1944, he bought two suits, rented a room in Harlem, and took a job as a dishwasher again. But now he felt differently about himself. He had begun to believe in the American Dream; he wanted to become famous and successful. His army comrades had talked constantly about their futures. Like them, Poitier started to set goals for himself. He had great confidence in his abilities, and he was not hampered by a fear of failure. Whatever he did not know how to do, he believed he could learn by trying.

One day, as he was browsing through *The Amsterdam News*, a Harlem newspaper, looking through the want ad listings for chauffeurs, porters, and janitors, he noticed an article entitled, "Actors Wanted by Little Theatre Group." He had never thought about being an actor before. He had never even been to a play. He had been to the movies, however, and he had some vague notions about what actors did. "I thought that actors made good money and I wanted to make money," he said later, recalling his reaction to the article, which mentioned auditions for students

Actor and director Frederick O'Neal (seated) witnessed Poitier's first acting audition, at the American Negro Theatre.

41

at the American Negro Theatre in Harlem. He was looking to do something more challenging than cleaning pots.

Clutching the article in his hand, Poitier arrived on the doorstep of a library on 135th Street and Lenox Avenue, in whose basement the American Negro Theatre was housed. Frederick O'Neal, one of the founders and managers of the theater, met Poitier at the door, handed him a script, and invited him onto the stage to read.

Poitier had never been on a stage before and had no idea what a script was. Even worse, he still could only read with extreme difficulty, and he spoke with a heavily intonated Bahamian accent. O'Neal stopped Poitier abruptly after just a few moments. Screaming that Poitier was wasting his time, he told the young man to get off the stage and find a job as a dishwasher. With such a thick accent, the stage manager told him, he could never become an actor.

Poitier was devastated by O'Neal's blunt critique of his abilities. He went home and thought about what the stage manager had said. After a little reflection, he decided that O'Neal had been right. He had read badly, and if he did not do something to improve himself, he would never be employed in anything other than menial work. "Had I accepted the rejection as my fate, I would have been hung in a kind of abyss of never really being able to reach beyond my grasp," he said. "I saw clearly that this was a crossroad and that I had to make a dramatic choice."

Within days of the audition, Poitier bought himself a radio and embarked upon a program of self-improvement that was to last for more than six months. Every night after work, he would turn on the radio and, starting at the top of the dial, tune in to different stations and imitate everything he heard. He would listen, then talk, listen, then talk. Soon, he began to lose his Bahamian accent.

While following this program to improve his speaking, Poitier worked on his literacy skills. He brought a newspaper to his job every day and read during lulls in his work. An old man who worked in the kitchen offered to help him with his studies, and Poitier's reading abilities began to improve rapidly. He struggled valiantly with silent letters, abbreviations, homonyms, and stressed and unstressed syllables until he was confident of his proficiency in the English language.

By April 1946, Poitier felt ready to return for another audition at the American Negro Theatre, which had moved into a larger space on 127th Street in Harlem and had grown substantially in reputation. This time 75 other prospective student actors were waiting to read, and Poitier saw that all of them were studying scenes from plays. He, on the other hand, had brought along a copy of *True Confessions* magazine, and he was planning to read one of the lurid stories in it for his audition. As he sat waiting for his turn, he wondered where the other applicants had found the scripts from which they were preparing, and he noticed that everyone was dressed very casually. In contrast, he was wearing his best brown suit, with a brown tie and matching brown shoes and socks.

Finally, Poitier was called to the stage and asked to stand beneath two bright spotlights. Feeling self-conscious and acutely embarrassed by his suit and his *True Confessions* magazine, he began to read a soppy story about two lovers, told from the woman's point of view. The audience began to twitter. Then, mercifully, Osceola Archer, the drama coach, stopped him and asked him to do an improvisation, pretending that he was in a jungle.

Although Poitier was relieved by the interruption, he did not understand what an improvisation was. He stood frozen on the stage, unsure of what to do next. At last, he turned his back to the audience, then swung around and began an imitation of a James

Poitier credits film star Jimmy Cagney (right) as the inspiration for his first theater improvisation. Asked to pretend during his audition that he was a soldier in the jungle, Poitier instead acted out a scene that he remembered from a Cagney movie.

Cagney gangster role. Pretending he had been shot, he toppled over but propped himself up with his hands a few inches from the floor so that he would not get his suit dirty.

One week later, to his complete astonishment, Poitier received an invitation from Abram Hill, the director of the American Negro Theatre, to join the theater school on a trial basis for three months. Forty applicants had passed the auditions, but all of them had been women. The theater needed male students and was willing to take a chance on Poitier.

Poitier felt proud and excited. He believed he had proved to himself and Frederick O'Neal that he could be an actor. Packing boxes at a shirt factory during the day, he attended classes at the theater every night. There he took courses in the fundamentals of acting, body movement, mime, diction, play directions, and other subjects. He began to like what he was doing, which in a way surprised him. He had started his program of self-improvement to overcome his initial failure, and his struggle to meet this self-imposed challenge had led him back to the American Negro

Abram Hill (second from left), president of the American Negro Theatre, poses with members of his staff. In 1946, he invited Poitier to join the theater on a trial basis.

Theatre. He had said to himself that once he had proved he could be an actor, he would move on to some other line of work. Yet he discovered that acting, which allowed him to play many different characters, gave him the opportunity to work at different aspects of his own character. He enjoyed this feeling of exploring that acting gave him.

When the three-month program was finished, the theater faculty asked Poitier to leave, deeming his progress insufficient to justify keeping him on at the school. He refused to accept that he had been given notice. By promising to serve as the theater's janitor for free, he bartered himself into a three-month extension. Hill clearly was impressed by Poitier's determination.

So began Poitier's acting career. He made an immediate impact at the theater once he settled down and began to make a serious attempt to learn about the acting profession. Earle Hyman, who worked with Poitier in 1946, remembered him as a "jack-in-the-box." Hyman said, "I remember thinking, 'Oh God, why doesn't he sit down. He's everywhere.' I was amazed when I first saw him act. All that energy was there, but it was controlled and channelled and beautifully ordered."

Poitier quickly made an impression on the other students, too. When Osceola Archer chose *Days of Our Youth* as the major student production of the semester, everyone, including Poitier, expected him to play the lead. He felt angry when he learned that Harry Belafonte, another young aspiring actor from the Caribbean, was going to play the role. Poitier was even more annoyed when he learned that Belafonte was not yet a student at the school. The episode created a rivalry between Poitier and the lighter-skinned Belafonte that was to last for many years. At the time, Poitier believed he was the victim of a certain bias against dark-skinned blacks that was shared by many middle-class members of the black community.

Succumbing to pressure from students and other members of the company, Archer finally agreed to let Poitier understudy Belafonte's role. It was a fortuitous decision for Poitier. Belafonte was ill and could not attend a rehearsal on the night that James Light, who had directed the original production of *Days of Our Youth*, was in the audience. A prominent director on Broadway, New York's theater district, Light was so impressed by Poitier's acting that he cast him as Polydorus in an all-black Broadway production of *Lysistrata*. This play was a modern adaptation of the ancient Greek playwright Aristophanes' comedy about the women of Athens, who refuse to sleep with their men until peace between the warring cities of Athens and Sparta has been declared.

Poitier has described the rehearsal period for his professional debut as four of the most enjoyable weeks of his life. It was the first time he earned money acting, and he subsequently decided to join the Actors' Equity Association, the union for professional performers in the theater.

On opening night, Poitier paced backstage, nervously practicing until he knew perfectly the 12 lines he was to speak. Nervousness soon turned to stage fright. When he went out on the stage, he could only talk in a whisper and he was trembling noticeably. He ran off the stage before his scene ended, believing he had ruined the show.

The reviews of the play stated that the production of *Lysistrata* was a failure. However, Poitier's performance was cited as being memorable and highly comic. Poitier felt that the comedy was purely accidental, a result of the paralytic stage fright that had made him fluff his lines and run off the stage. Nonetheless, the American Negro Theatre management was impressed enough to offer him a job as understudy in their touring show, *Anna Lucasta*, a play about a group of sailors who work on the Brooklyn waterfront. Beginning in 1946, Poitier served a three-year apprenticeship in a traveling theater show, which ended in 1949, when he was 22 years old. These were the years when he learned to act and to work with a company.

This was also the time when Poitier first fell deeply in love. During the show's run in Boston, Massachusetts, he met Ann Gurdine, the daughter of Colonel Ned Gurdine, one of the highest ranking black officers in the army. Poitier was entranced with Ann, whom he still describes as his "dream girl." The young couple saw each other daily during the few weeks Poitier was in Boston. They spoke of getting married,

but her parents were opposed to the idea of their daughter marrying a poorly paid actor. Poitier reluctantly left Boston, and he returned there often during the following years to visit Ann. However, they eventually drifted apart. His chosen profession and her parents' objections made a future together seem impossible.

Speaking of his drive to succeed as an actor, Poitier said, "My eye was fastened to the possibility that somewhere in those years my dreams could materialize and I could shoot through a barrier into uncharted waters where no black actor had never been before." His vision of where his career might lead him had broadened, taking his mind off his failed love affair with Ann Gurdine. He was reaching out for success and public recognition, and he was looking toward Hollywood. ✿

Poitier's classmates at the American Negro Theatre school included actor Harry Belafonte (right). Ruby Dee and Earle Hyman were other notable talents who attended the school.

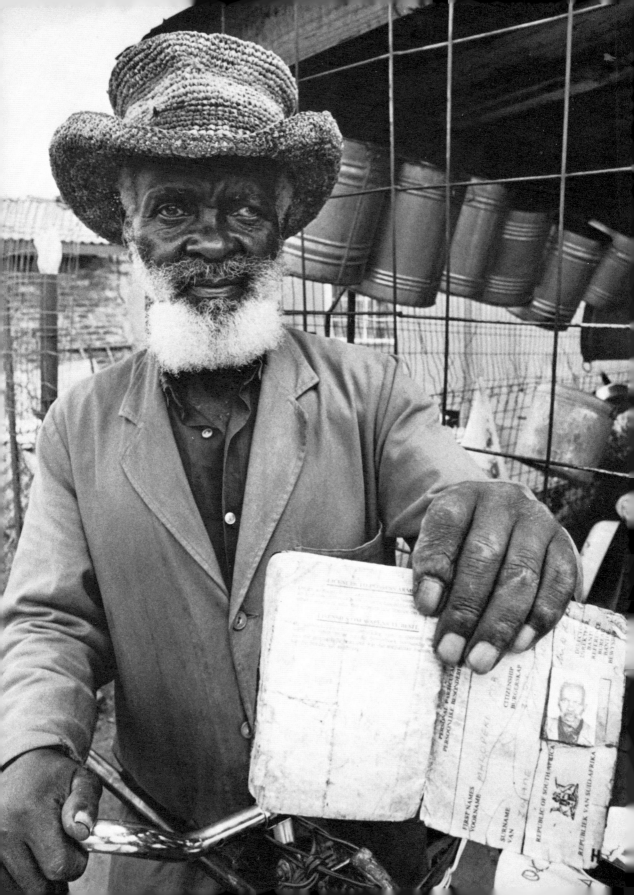

5

ON TO
HOLLYWOOD

———————— ✿ ————————

WHEN THE SHOW *Anna Lucasta* finally folded
in 1949 after a three-year national tour, Poitier returned to New York. Only seven years had passed
since his departure from Nassau, yet the 22 year old
was already a professional actor who had gained the
attention of a small circle of theater critics, actors,
and directors.

Energetic and ambitious, Poitier seemed unintim-
idated by the odds facing any black actor trying to
find major roles on the stage or screen. Perhaps this
was because he was from the Bahamas and he had
not faced the overt bigotry that many of his black
American colleagues had lived with while they were
growing up.

Upon his return to New York, Poitier heard that
auditions were being given for a new Broadway show,
Lost in the Stars, a musical based on Alan Paton's
poignant novel about South Africa, *Cry, the Beloved
Country*. Poitier was the only actor to arrive at the
audition without an agent, and he was told that there
was little chance that he would be allowed to try out
for a part. Undaunted, he approached one of the
agents who was present at the audition, Bill Nichols
of the Jules Ziegler Agency, and convinced the man
to represent him. Both men were pleasantly surprised
when Poitier was offered a role in the show. In one
afternoon, he had landed himself an agent and a part
in a Broadway play.

*A native South African displays
his passbook. Legal documents
such as this one have been used
by the South African government
to regulate the movements of
blacks within the country.*

Meanwhile, Poitier heard about another audition, this one for a movie that was to be filmed in Hollywood, California. Even though he already had a part in *Lost in the Stars*, he decided to go to the audition to gain more experience. He had recently appeared in two short films, one a 10-minute religious film called *From Whom Cometh My Help* and the other an Army Signal Corps film called *Sepia Cinderella*. He had discovered that he felt even more comfortable in front of a camera than he did on the stage. The audition across town was especially tempting because it was a major production, a Twentieth Century Fox film called *No Way Out*. The popular actor Richard Widmark, who was best known for his portrayal of killers and hoodlums, was signed to play the lead role in the film, and it was to be directed by veteran Hollywood producer Joseph L. Mankiewicz.

To his amazement, Poitier was offered an important part in the film. He ran over to the Jules Ziegler Agency to tell them the good news, but he had to admit that there was a difficulty. He had two job offers, one of which he would have to turn down. Used to these kinds of problems, Ziegler immediately called the producer of *Lost in the Stars* and got Poitier released from his commitment.

Shortly thereafter, Poitier left for California on a cross-country train called *The Twentieth Century Limited*. The streamlined cars and over-grand title captured his excited mood and high spirits as he set out for Hollywood. Representatives from the studio met him at the train station in California and drove him to a comfortable apartment hotel in Westwood, near Hollywood. Poitier had never experienced such luxury before. He was mesmerized by the clear blue sky and clean streets. It reminded him of the Bahamas. "Everybody seemed to be on vacation," he observed.

When he began to look around Westwood more closely, he noticed that he was the only black person

While Poitier worked on the film version of Cry, the Beloved Country *in South Africa, he witnessed the horror and misery of the country's apartheid system.*

among many whites. Once at the studio, he was struck even more forcefully that there were almost no members of any minority groups working on the set, even though the film he was about to make dealt forthrightly with racial prejudice.

Poitier's first feature movie, *No Way Out*, is a classic among a genre of post–World War II movies that attempted to portray racial tensions in a realistic manner. In the film, Poitier plays the part of Dr. Luther Brooks, the only black intern in a large inner-city hospital. The doctor is subjected to racial insults from his medical colleagues as well as his patients. When a man whom Brooks suspects has been wrongly diagnosed dies while the doctor is preparing to operate on him, the man's brother, Ray Biddle, played by Richard Widmark, starts a campaign against the "black killer." Biddle refuses to allow an autopsy to be performed, which would prove the young doctor's innocence, and instead instigates a race riot. Finally, the calm, dignified Brooks proves his innocence and convinces the doctors with whom he works that a black doctor should be permitted to work on white as well as on black patients.

Poitier prepared for the demanding role by observing interns at Los Angeles General Hospital. He also sought the advice of his new friend and mentor, Richard Widmark, while studying his lines. Widmark and his wife, Jean, were the first Hollywood residents to welcome Poitier into their home.

When Poitier saw the rushes—the unedited film of his first day's shooting—he felt a little perplexed. He could hardly recognize himself. However, the critics were ultimately impressed by his performance as a doctor who must deal with racial prejudice on both a public and professional level.

After completing the shooting, Poitier flew back to New York in mid-1950. It was his first ride in an airplane, and his spirits were flying high as well. He

had $3,000 in his pocket and a recommendation to see Zoltan Korda, an English director, who was preparing to make the film version of Cry, the Beloved Country. When Poitier reached New York, he hardly had time to unpack his suitcase and put his money in the bank. Korda wanted him to come to London, England, at once to audition for the part of a young black South African minister. After the audition, Korda offered Poitier the role.

Because the film was not set to begin production for a few months, Poitier decided to take advantage of this break in his schedule and went to see his

Poitier and Canada Lee (right) played the roles of preachers in South Africa in the 1951 film Cry, the Beloved Country. Poitier received widespread acclaim for his powerful performance, yet he was not offered another substantial film role until three years later.

parents. Strangely, he had not written to his family since his arrival in Miami eight years before. Although he knew that his parents had meant well when they had sent him away from home, he may still have harbored some resentments against them for cutting him loose at such an early age. His first few years in the United States had been difficult, and his struggle for survival had used up all of his energy. Now, more confident and with some money to show for his struggles, he wanted to see his parents again and apologize to them for being such a neglectful son.

The more Poitier thought about his lack of contact with his parents, the more distressed and guilty he felt. Family members who moved to the United States were expected to send money home to their relatives, but he had never done so. He had never written to his mother because he was afraid that she would be disappointed in him. Therefore, his pilgrimage back to Nassau in 1951 was important for his growth as an actor and a man. He had to go back in order to see how far he had traveled and to understand the gift that his parents had given him when they had set him loose.

Arriving unannounced one evening at his parents' home, Poitier was deeply moved as he looked into the familiar old house and saw his mother and father sitting quietly at their kitchen table, upon which a kerosene lamp was burning. He would later write, "The Poitier family has been reduced to these two people in their twilight years, their children all gone—some into marriage, others off into worlds where Evelyn and Reginald cannot follow. And the youngest of them all—the baby of the bunch—has simply disappeared somewhere in America nearly eight years ago."

Poitier's parents barely recognized their youngest son: Since leaving the Bahamas, he had grown to a height of six feet two inches. They greeted him with

At the age of 22, Poitier returned to his childhood home in Nassau to reestablish contact with his parents.

hugs and kisses, and Poitier saw that his father was in poor health. He tried to explain to his parents what kind of work he was doing in the United States. This was somewhat difficult because Evelyn Poitier had never seen a movie.

After spending several more days meeting with his brothers, sisters, and other relatives, Poitier returned to New York. He gave his parents most of the money he had earned for his part in *No Way Out*, and he promised his family and himself that he would keep in close touch with them. Later, he reflected on how hard it had been for him to accept that his parents' home had an outhouse and no electricity. He hoped that they had not been hurt that he had stayed in a hotel.

No Way Out opened in a Nassau theater a few months later. Poitier's parents were invited to attend as guests of honor, but Reginald was too frail. Evelyn went to the showing, but she had difficulty understanding that the events shown on the screen were not real. At the end of the picture, when Luther Brooks is attacked by Ray Biddle, Poitier's mother stood up in the crowded theater and yelled out, "Hit him back, baby! Hit him back!"

Once more in New York, Poitier prepared for his departure to Johannesburg, South Africa, where *Cry, the Beloved Country* was to be filmed. In South Africa, the white minority population ruled over a much larger black population. To comply with the racially discriminatory laws of South Africa's brutal apartheid system, Poitier had to sign papers indenturing himself to the director, Zoltan Korda. This meant that Poitier would be bound in service to Korda for a specified term. The system of indenturing was little better than slavery, and it was illegal in the United States. Poitier would not have any personal freedoms, such as the right to quit his job. Korda insisted that the contract was a mere formality that must be recognized in order for them to make their important film.

In later years, Poitier would be criticized for working in South Africa. In response to these attacks, he said that *Cry, the Beloved Country* "gave me the chance to say some things about apartheid that needed saying. . . . I wanted to project what it was like to be black under the iron heel of a vicious racist white minority. . . . Sure, it was humiliation to have to indenture myself, but sometimes you have to take a punch to land a harder one."

In some ways, the trip to South Africa was a continuation of Poitier's pilgrimage to Nassau. He and Canada Lee, who played the lead role in the movie, were forced to share a farmhouse on the outskirts of Johannesburg because blacks were not allowed to stay in a hotel in the city. The farmhouse overlooked the shanty slums where Johannesburg's black population lived. The walls of the houses were made of corrugated metal sheets, with burlap sacks used to cover windows and doors. Poitier saw a distinct relation between the miserable conditions that blacks were forced to endure in South Africa and the poverty he had just seen in his parents' neighborhood in Nassau.

Poitier left South Africa with an increased awareness of the legacy of colonialism, something that the oppressed black people in South Africa shared with the descendants of slaves in the West Indies and the United States. Unlike militant black Americans who in the coming years would resort to violent means to correct social injustices, Poitier chose to view the racial scene in the more hopeful manner that would be expressed by Martin Luther King, Jr. "I came back," Poitier said, "pondering the validity of 'fight fire with fire, hate with hate.' I finally resolved it by deciding that not only was hatred alien to my nature, but it was evil."

Cry, the Beloved Country is a moving story of love and forgiveness. It follows the journey of the Reverend Kumalo, a preacher from a rural area of South

Poitier and his first wife, Juanita, in the mid-1950s.

Africa, who travels to the city of Johannesburg to search for his sister and his son. When he arrives, he discovers that his sister has turned to prostitution in order to survive and that his son has murdered the son of a white farmer. Poitier plays the part of the young Reverend Msimangu, who comes to the aid of Kumalo, who is played by Canada Lee.

The film opened to excellent critical reviews in 1951. With more good notices under his belt, Poitier hoped that he would never again have to take a job as a dishwasher. But he was not yet earning enough money to sustain himself between acting jobs and he was forced to take on menial work to survive. He soon had more responsibilities to think about. In September 1951, he married Juanita Hardy, a model and dancer, with whom he fell in love soon after his return from South Africa. They had been introduced by one of his friends, Bill Greaves, who had shown Poitier three magazines—*Ebony*, *Sepia*, and *Our World*—on whose covers Juanita Hardy had just appeared. When Poitier said he would like to meet the beautiful woman, Greaves, who knew Hardy, arranged the introduction. After a few months of courtship, they celebrated a wedding ceremony in a church in Harlem. However, Poitier could not afford to bring his parents to the United States to see him get married.

Writing home to his parents about his bride, Poitier described the steadying and calming influence that Juanita had on his life. Realizing that the lives of most actors were unpredictable and insecure, he fully appreciated how important it was to have someone like Juanita by his side. After the wedding, she took menial jobs in between modeling assignments to help make ends meet, while he alternated between dishwashing and construction work. Their spare money was spent on Poitier's classes at the Paul Mann Actors Workshop in Manhattan. The young couple moved to Long Island, where the first of their four daughters, Beverly, was born on July 4, 1952.

With the arrival of a new baby, earning steady money became even more of a necessity. While appearing in a short-lived play called *Detective Story* at the Apollo Theater in Harlem, Poitier met Johnny Newton, who worked in a local bar. The two became friends and partners in a restaurant called Ribs in the Ruff, which featured Poitier's special Caribbean barbecue sauce. At the time, opening a restaurant seemed like a good idea, but during the next few years much of the money Poitier made from his performances in films and plays went into the business. That restaurant and three others that he and Newton opened were to become a source of irritation and debt until he finally closed them in 1957.

From 1951 to 1954, Poitier was able to get only two small film roles. In 1952, he appeared in *Red Ball Express*, a war film about the exploits of the famous World War II army trucking supply unit that was composed mainly of blacks. Then, in 1954, he had a part in *Go, Man, Go!*, a film about the formation of the Harlem Globetrotters, the team of touring black basketball players known for its amazing stunts and humorous pranks on the court. His appearances in the two films amounted to only eight weeks' worth of work. It was a difficult time for him, and he later remarked, "I did a great deal of fretting and worrying that eventually crystallized into an ulcer condition."

Reflecting on the obstacles that he had to face in finding work after his first two successful films, *No Way Out* and *Cry, the Beloved Country*, Poitier has pointed out that the movie studios only considered him for roles that had to be played by blacks. He was never asked to audition for parts that could be played by either white or black actors.

In 1954, when an interviewer asked Poitier why he had lately done so little acting work, he said, "Hollywood as a rule doesn't want to portray us [black people] as anything but butlers, chauffeurs, gardeners or maids. They just don't want to make us part of contemporary American life. As an actor, if I have the ability, all I ask is the opportunity. When it is denied to me because of my color then I can't help feeling resentful."

This was a brave statement for a young black actor to make at that time. The broadcast and entertainment industry had come under increasing pressure

from Senator Joseph McCarthy's Senate Permanent Investigating Sub-Committee, which, along with the House Un-American Activities Committee (HUAC), conducted a series of hearings in the early 1950s in an attempt to show that communists and members of other left-wing organizations were exerting a strong influence on the U.S. government and other parts of American society. The HUAC concerned itself primarily with the entertainment industry. Many Hollywood directors, screenwriters, and actors were called in front of the committee and accused of being communists or questioned about their associations with people who were alleged to be spies and agents of the Soviet Union.

In the late 1940s, the fear of communist conspiracies began to grip American society. Senator Joseph McCarthy (shown here conferring with Senator Robert Kennedy) was instrumental in the congressional crusade to identify communists and their sympathizers.

An atmosphere of near hysteria pervaded the entertainment field during these years, even though most of the accusations of communism were baseless. McCarthy and his supporters viewed anyone who called for reforms in American society as being unpatriotic and subversive. Black actors were considered particularly suspect, especially if they were outspoken.

Because of his forthright statements to the press about the lack of opportunities for black actors, Poitier had to face the fact that he might be blacklisted, which meant being barred from being accepted for any roles on the stage or screen. The heads of the broadcasting and entertainment industries subscribed to a newsletter called "Counterattack," which listed performers suspected of having communist sympathies.

Whether Poitier's name actually appeared on the "Counterattack" list is uncertain, but in 1954 he was asked to sign a "loyalty oath," a statement that he had no intentions of overthrowing the U.S. government, before he was allowed to accept a role in a film called *Blackboard Jungle*. The HUAC charged that Poitier was closely connected to certain suspect members of the black community, people such as the famous singer and actor Paul Robeson and the actor Canada Lee, with whom Poitier had appeared in *Cry, the Beloved Country*. Poitier had a great deal of respect for both of these men. It was also noted in his file that he had appeared at Actors' Equity meetings and demanded that black actors be given equal rights.

Poitier was given a leading role in *Blackboard Jungle*, though he claims that he refused to sign the loyalty oath and that a compromise was reached that enabled him to work. He was nearly 28 years old at the time he appeared in the film, yet he was still able to give a convincing performance as the high school student Gregory Miller in a realistic drama about an inner-city school. Poitier's character is a tough boy who, like the other students, has contempt for his

Usually a jocular and witty man in public, renowned singer and actor Paul Robeson had no smiles for the House Un-American Activities Committee in 1956. He told them, "You want to shut up every Negro who has the courage to stand up and fight for the rights of his people, for the rights of workers."

The 1955 film Blackboard Jungle, *a harrowing portrait of rebellious youths, catapulted Poitier into the front ranks of America's serious, young actors. He is shown here with actor Glenn Ford.*

idealistic teacher Richard Dadier, who is played by Glenn Ford. The film traces Miller's growing respect for Dadier and his courage in protecting the teacher against the physical attack of the toughest kid in the school, played by Vic Morrow.

Blackboard Jungle was very successful at the box office, and Poitier was acclaimed for his sensitive portrayal of a troubled young man. Director Richard Brooks attributed Poitier's outstanding performance to "an amazingly profound and sympathetic understanding of human virtues." A controversy arose when the State Department attempted to block the distribution of the film overseas, stating that it showed America in a bad light. The publicity generated from the debate undoubtedly helped Poitier's career and made him more visible to agents and producers.

In 1956, Poitier went to Georgia for a part in a children's film, *Goodbye, My Lady*, which attracted little attention. Then, back in New York, he received a phone call from agent Martin Baum, asking if he would be interested in a part in a film about a black man who is victimized by gangsters. After reading the script, Poitier decided against taking the role. He told Baum that he would not accept parts that had no special significance to them. Stunned by the actor's courage and integrity, Baum told Poitier that he wanted to be his agent. "Anybody as crazy as you are," Baum said, "I want to represent them."

After Poitier signed with the energetic and aggressive Baum, his career began to enjoy great success. The turning point came in 1957, when Poitier appeared on television for the first time in a production of a Robert Alan Aurthur play, *A Man Is Ten Feet Tall*. The story is about two dockworkers, one white and one black, whose friendship is threatened by a bullying bigot. The production was given a national, prime-time showing by the NBC television network. After it was broadcast, NBC received calls from many

The actor's family at home: Poitier and his first wife, Juanita, with their daughters Sherri (on her father's lap), Pamela, and Beverly (right).

enraged viewers, who protested the decision to allow Poitier's character to have a white girlfriend. Hilda Simms, who played the part of the girlfriend, was actually a light-skinned black actress, but the controversy was a measure of the state of race relations at that time.

In 1957, Poitier also appeared in the film version of *A Man Is Ten Feet Tall*. The motion picture was called *Edge of the City* and was produced by David Susskind, who was instrumental in helping to create many new job opportunities for black actors in New York's entertainment industry. Poitier next made three films in quick succession: *Something of Value*, *Mark of the Hawk*, and *Band of Angels*. His explosive performance in *Something of Value*, a drama about an interracial friendship during the Mau Mau uprising in East Africa, won special praise.

During this time, Poitier was often away from his family, and stresses were beginning to appear in his marriage. While Juanita stayed at home raising Beverly as well as their other two daughters, Pamela and Sherri, Poitier traveled to California and Africa to appear in films with such stars as Rock Hudson, Eartha Kitt, and Clark Gable. Juanita had little interest in the entertainment world, and she and Poitier found as time wore on that they had less and less to talk about. Deciding that he wanted his children to grow up in a community with diverse cultural influences, he moved his family to a comfortable house in a multiracial, working-class section of Mount Vernon, New York, a suburb of New York City. Privately, he was hoping that a change of scene would also help his marriage.

Showered with critical acclaim for his acting in *Something of Value* and *A Man Is Ten Feet Tall*, Poitier was beginning to feel the strains of celebrity. The adjustment to becoming a star was not altogether easy. However, the way to escape from the pressures at home was becoming clear to him: The door to Hollywood was opening wide.

6

THE
ACADEMY
AWARD

THE CIVIL RIGHTS movement was beginning to gather momentum just as Poitier was catapulted to stardom by his appearances in several films in the late 1950s and early 1960s. His rise to fame during this period was not accidental. Hollywood was beginning to take a strong interest in the box office potential of films dealing with racial problems, and Poitier was quickly becoming the most powerful black screen actor. While civil rights marchers demonstrated for integrated schools and transportation systems in cities throughout the South, Poitier's film roles were presenting blacks as models of proud and dynamic men.

In 1958, Poitier appeared with Tony Curtis in *The Defiant Ones*, a story about a pair of southern convicts, one white and one black, who escape from a prison van. Chained together, the two men are totally reliant on each other for their survival. The script appealed to producer-director Stanley Kramer, who was known for his courage in tackling difficult subject matter. Poitier has recalled that Kramer was "just itching to address head on those issues other producers were inclined to dance around."

Thanks to the insistence of Tony Curtis, Poitier shared costar billing. He won the New York Film Critics Circle Award for Best Actor for his portrayal of the convict Noah Cullen. "I think it [*The Defiant Ones*] has universal applicability," Poitier told a re-

In the 1958 film The Defiant Ones, *both Poitier and costar Tony Curtis (center) won an Academy Award nomination for Best Actor for their portrayals of escaped convicts. Although neither actor won the award, the racially charged movie was named Best Picture of the year.*

porter after receiving the award, "because whether we like it or not, we are chained together and if one of us drowns the other one is going down too."

Critics and directors who had already begun to appreciate Poitier's range as an actor pointed to *The Defiant Ones* as confirmation of the 31-year-old actor's potential of becoming one of the great screen stars. Kramer compared him to his contemporary, actor Marlon Brando: "Like Brando, he can be a pathetic and even pitiful character, and then he can go instantly to moments of overwhelming and savage emotional power." Both Poitier and Curtis were nominated for the Academy Award for Best Actor but lost to David Niven. Still, Poitier's selection as one of the five finalists for the nation's top acting award broke another barrier for black actors. (The black actress Dorothy Dandridge previously had been nominated for the Best Actress Award for her role in *Carmen Jones*.)

Producer Samuel Goldwyn was bombarded with objections by several prominent civil rights groups when he proposed to make a film version of Porgy and Bess. *These groups felt that the opera perpetuated a negative, stereotyped image of blacks.*

With his earnings from *The Defiant Ones*, Poitier was at last able to buy his parents a comfortable home in Nassau and to provide them with a monthly allowance for the few remaining years of their lives. This, he felt, was his greatest reward from working on the film.

Although Poitier wished to be viewed as a talented actor rather than just as a talented black actor, that he was one of the leading representatives for blacks in the entertainment industry placed additional burdens on him. During this period of turbulence and change in American society, Poitier had to pay close attention to the black community's opinion about the films he was working on. "Suddenly, decisions of a very political nature were on my doorstep," he wrote about the furor that broke over his next film, *Porgy and Bess*, which was based on the 1935 opera by George Gershwin about the black community living on Catfish Row in Charleston, South Carolina.

Poitier was cast as Porgy, a drunken cripple who is the brunt of all the jokes in the neighborhood. He falls in love with the beautiful Bess (played by Dorothy Dandridge), who takes refuge with him after her lover, a murderer named Crown, leaves town. When Crown returns, Porgy kills him and is arrested by the police. Eventually, Porgy is released and goes off in search of Bess, who has gone to New York with the drug pusher Sportin' Life (played by Sammy Davis, Jr.).

Samuel Goldwyn, the head of Metro-Goldwyn-Mayer studios and the producer of the film, had a very clear idea of how he hoped to bring the opera to the screen. He did not intend to change any of the original stereotyped images of the happy-go-lucky black men and women on Catfish Row who sing and fight and idle away their days playing dice and falling in love.

Poitier was away in the Caribbean making a film called *Virgin Island* when an agent who was temporarily representing him was called into Goldwyn's office. Without getting the actor's consent, a verbal commitment was made by this agent for Poitier to play Porgy. When he returned to the United States, he was immediately besieged by civil rights groups pressuring him to back out of the commitment. Other black actors and actresses were also encouraged to boycott the film.

Goldwyn had Poitier trapped. A verbal commitment had been made, and in Hollywood that is as good as a signed contract. Poitier knew that his film career would be in jeopardy if he refused to play Porgy—especially because Goldwyn was one of the most powerful men in Hollywood and he could ensure that Poitier never got another screen role. Trying to regain some control over a bad situation, Poitier asked for the right to make changes in the script, but Goldwyn refused this request.

Reluctantly, Poitier decided to play Porgy. Once he succumbed to Goldwyn's pressure, the other actors ended their boycott. However, the set of *Porgy and Bess* was, said one observer, "like a guerilla war." The film's director, the dictatorial Otto Preminger, screamed insults at actress Dorothy Dandridge while the rest of the cast stood by helpless and paralyzed. Dandridge did not have the self-confidence to challenge Preminger. However, when Preminger began to abuse Poitier, the actor walked off the set. He returned only after Preminger apologized to him and promised to treat him with respect.

The film was eventually completed, but it took its toll on the members of the cast. Poitier, Ruby Dee, Sammy Davis, Jr., Dorothy Dandridge, Diahann Carroll, and the other performers were criticized by much of the black community for participating in a film that was said to be demeaning to blacks. Although Poitier recognized that many people would

dislike the film, he believed that he and the other performers had brought some dimension to roles that had been mere caricatures in the script. Film critics commended him for investing the crippled Porgy with a quiet dignity and strength, and although the tone-deaf Poitier did not sing any of the opera's songs, he spent many hours of practice to make sure that his lip-syncing was exact.

While Poitier was working on *Porgy and Bess*, he fell in love with the elegant, beautiful actress Diahann Carroll. Feeling guilty about their affair, he nonetheless had to recognize that his marriage had been deteriorating gradually for years. He was extremely troubled by the thought of leaving his children, and he was angry that he and Juanita had not been able to reconcile their differences. For the time being, he decided to move out of the house. Later, he would make an attempt to patch up his marriage, and he and Juanita would have one more child, a daughter named Gina. But after a long separation, the two were officially divorced some years later.

During the making of Porgy and Bess, *actress Diahann Carroll (right) became involved with Poitier both on-screen and off-screen.*

Lorraine Hansberry (shown here) wrote the stirring drama A Raisin in the Sun when she was 28 years old. Poitier escorted the young playwright onto the stage to acknowledge a standing ovation after the show's Broadway opening proved to be a triumph.

Diahann Carroll and Poitier began a relationship that was to last for nine years. Carroll was to become famous for her starring role in "Julia," a television situation comedy that surmounted significant racial hurdles in the late 1960s when it became the first successful show built around a black performer. Until "Julia" became popular, few advertisers were willing to sponsor a show with black stars because they knew that many of the network's affiliates in the South would refuse to broadcast it. As pioneers in breaking down racial barriers in the television and film industries, Poitier and Carroll had much in common.

In 1960, Poitier returned to the stage for the first time in 10 years to perform the part of Walter Lee in *A Raisin in the Sun*, Lorraine Hansberry's gripping drama about a poor black family in Chicago, Illinois, that must decide how to use the money received from the recently deceased father's life insurance policy. The play was an immediate hit and attracted an unusually large integrated audience during its Broadway run. Many people from Harlem who had never been to the theater before came to see the play.

Poitier identified strongly with the character of Walter Lee, whom he described as a man who "has an obsession—he wants to and has not been able to carve for himself a badge of distinction. The only acceptable one, the only one he recognizes, would be some material symbol of his life's worth." But Poitier was not entirely happy with the play. He did not think that the story should be told from the mother's point of view, and he told Lorraine Hansberry during trial performances in New Haven, Connecticut, and Chicago that he thought Walter Lee, the play's strongest black male role, would be viewed as too negative a character if the script was not changed. Poitier's attempt to tamper with Hansberry's creative vision brought charges against him of exhibiting egotistical, "star" behavior.

The script was not changed, and Poitier went on to appear in the film version of *A Raisin in the Sun* in 1961. However, his relationship with Lorraine Hansberry remained strained until they had a reconciliation a few years later, shortly before the playwright's tragic early death.

From 1960 to 1962, Poitier had parts in three other films besides *A Raisin in the Sun*. In *All the Young Men*, he played a marine sergeant who commands a platoon that comes under heavy fire during a Korean War battle. He then linked up with Diahann Carroll, Paul Newman, and Joanne Woodward in *Paris Blues*, a story about two American jazz musicians living in France. In *Pressure Point*, another Stanley Kramer production, he played a psychiatrist who has to battle racial prejudice on his job at a prison. The films gained Poitier more public notice, but they received lukewarm reviews from the critics.

The 1961 film version of A Raisin in the Sun *featured Poitier as Walter Lee Younger and actress Claudia McNeil (left) as his mother. Prior to making the film, Poitier starred in the same role in the Broadway production of the drama.*

Poitier attended the Cannes Film Festival in France for the premiere of A Raisin in the Sun.

Voicing his opinion about the script of *A Raisin in the Sun* soon proved to be the first stirring of a new spirit in Poitier. Although he was still at the mercy of Hollywood's studio bosses, he was becoming increasingly influential as an actor. Accordingly, he grew determined to overturn the film industry's system of institutionalized racism, which excluded blacks from participating in any of the decisions involved in the development of a film.

Poitier had a chance to air his views when he was called to testify in front of the Committee on Education and Labor headed by Harlem congressman Adam Clayton Powell, Jr. The committee was investigating discrimination in the entertainment industry. Poitier said, "It's no great joy to me to be used as a symbol, an example of how they [the leaders of the film industry] don't really discriminate."

But he was also a symbol of real black achievement. When he accepted the Academy Award for Best Actor on the night of April 13, 1964, for his portrayal of Homer Smith in *Lilies of the Field*, it was the culmination of years of effort, a moment charged both with historic significance and personal sadness for Poitier. His mother had died just a few weeks before the night of the ceremony, three years after the death of his father. Poitier greatly regretted that neither of them were present to celebrate his triumph in *Lilies of the Field*.

A low-budget film shot in just 14 days, *Lilies of the Field* is a simple story about a young drifter, the ex-soldier Homer Smith, who befriends a group of German nuns in the Arizona desert, eventually building them the chapel they so desperately want. The film's director, Ralph Nelson, was so moved by the tale of human goodness, hard work, and redemption that he put his own house up as collateral in order to make the movie. Poitier knew instinctively that *Lilies of the Field* would be a success and that the part of Homer Smith was a good vehicle for him. Unable to pay Poitier the salary to which he had become accustomed, Nelson offered Poitier a share of the profits. The deal ultimately worked out very well for Poitier.

Some cynics have suggested that if the civil rights movement had not been so popular with a large segment of the American public in 1964, Poitier would not have won the film academy's Oscar. But these sniping remarks cannot diminish Poitier's powerful, humorous, deeply human portrait of a man rediscovering a lost dream, "to make something with my own hands." In portraying Homer Smith on the screen, Poitier's own dream had come true. With the Oscar, he had become not just a star but a superstar, a person of stature and importance in Hollywood. ❧

In 1960, Congressman Adam Clayton Powell, Jr., became head of the House Committee on Education and Labor, which investigated discrimination in the entertainment industry. Poitier was asked to give testimony before the committee.

7
BREAKING DOWN THE BARRIERS

T HREE WEEKS AFTER receiving the Academy Award, Poitier returned to Nassau at the invitation of the Bahamian government to receive a hero's welcome. Crowds lining the route from the airport to the city waved banners proclaiming "Hail Sidney" and "Your Glory Is Ours." Poitier was overwhelmed by the celebration, calling it one of the most moving experiences of his life. "It rained," he said, "but I was bathed in love." The day was capped by a ceremony in the building that housed the Bahamian government, with the governor toasting Poitier's success in front of more than 200 guests.

Memories of his parents, family, and friends who had not escaped the poverty of Nassau made Poitier feel humble as well as proud. Winning the Academy Award had not swept away all of his fears about his future as an actor, but returning to the Bahamas did help him to become reacquainted with the people and places of his youth.

Back in the United States, Poitier began to accustom himself to his lofty position in the film world. However, he was deeply troubled by the contrast between his own success and the high level of unemployment among black actors. Commenting on his Academy Award victory, he told an interviewer, "I do hope there will be some residual benefits for other Negro actors, but I don't fool myself into thinking the effect will be vast."

Poitier with Elizabeth Hartman in the 1966 film A Patch of Blue, one of four films that he was asked to make in quick succession after winning the Academy Award.

Because of his widespread popularity, Poitier was able to press more strongly for a greater black presence in the film industry. However, no substantial improvements would occur until the late 1960s, when black producers and directors began to form their own production companies. Poitier's own positive effect on the changes within the film industry cannot be underestimated, despite his own modesty on the subject. He was in the right place at the right time, he insists, but that is not entirely true. In an era when many militant black groups were calling for racial separatism and a boycott of white-controlled industries and organizations, Poitier remained strongly committed to furthering better relationships between blacks and whites. Naturally, the heads of the film industry were more willing to comply with Poitier's demands than to bow to pressures from militant black groups.

Poitier felt these pressures, too, and they were not comfortable or easy to bear. Statements that he was the film studios' "token" black began appearing in the black press. The criticism reached a peak in an article printed in the *New York Times* in 1967, when black critic Clifford Mason called Poitier a "showcase nigger." Though troubled by these attacks, which he believed were malicious and untrue, Poitier was not swayed from his resolve to further integrate the film industry. He had already proven to Hollywood the economic drawing power a popular black actor could have with both black and white audiences. He was able to cross the color line, and if separatist blacks wanted to call him a "model integrationist," he would carry the label with pride, not shame. All told, most of the black community admired Poitier.

After Poitier's standout performance in *Lilies of the Field*, he began receiving offers of roles that were not specially designed for a black actor. In *The Bedford*

Incident, he was cast as a journalist who, while traveling on an American warship, discovers that the ship's captain (played by Richard Widmark) is dangerously unstable and intends to make an unprovoked attack on a Soviet submarine. *The Long Ships* pitted him in the role of a Muslim ruler against Richard Widmark's Viking adventurer. In *The Slender Thread*, Poitier played a hospital hotline attendant who tries to convince a desperate caller not to commit suicide. In 1966, he teamed with actor James Garner in *Duel at Diablo*, a western in which Poitier portrayed an ex-soldier and horse trader who becomes involved in an Indian uprising.

After Poitier won the Academy Award in 1964, he became a star of international stature. He is shown here in The Slender Thread, *having been cast as the lead even though the part was not designated for a black actor.*

Shelley Winters (left) and Elizabeth Hartman (center) appeared in A Patch of Blue with Poitier, who said, "My career was continuing to build in ways that would be advantageous to the black community and to other black actors."

Although these films were satisfying to Poitier in that they helped to break down racial barriers in the film industry, none of them stretched him artistically. By the time *Patch of Blue* was released in 1966, he was beginning to grapple with another issue—emphasizing the sexuality of black men and women on the screen. In *Patch of Blue*, he played the store clerk Gordon Ralfe, who befriends a young, blind white woman unaware that the man who is so kind to her is black. The woman's mother, a hard-bitten prostitute, tries to break up the friendship and reveals to her daughter that Ralfe is black. However, in the film, the relationship between Ralfe and the blind woman is never allowed to progress to romance and is kept antiseptically asexual.

In the films that he made prior to 1967, Poitier said, he "never worked in a man-woman relationship that was not symbolic. Either there were no women or there was a woman, but she was blind, or the relationship was of a nature that satisfied the taboos." Even Poitier had difficulty persuading the film studios to demolish this most tenacious of racial taboos.

After winning the Academy Award, Poitier was besieged with requests from black organizations. Increasingly, he was asked to appear at civil rights functions and to aid in fund-raising efforts. He had become friendly with the popular singer and actor Harry Belafonte, his old rival at the American Negro Theatre, who was actively involved in the civil rights cause.

On one occasion in the mid-1960s, Belafonte brought Poitier on a dangerous mission to Greenville, Mississippi, to deliver bail money to the Student Nonviolent Coordinating Committee (SNCC). The young men and women of the SNCC were leading a drive to ensure that blacks in the South were registered to vote. Yet many of them had been arrested by racist law officers. On the ride from the airport to Greenville, Poitier and Belafonte were almost run off the road by a car filled with Ku Klux Klan members. But Poitier was glad to lend his moral support to the students in Mississippi and to be able to play another part in the civil rights cause.

Poitier's next three films—all released in 1967, the year before civil rights leader Dr. Martin Luther King, Jr., was assassinated—reflected the nation's continuing obsession with unresolved racial issues. Poitier's film career had blossomed during the years that the civil rights movement came of age, and it was appropriate that at the age of 40 he should participate in three demanding film projects in which he played mature, accomplished black men. Diahann Carroll said of Poitier during this time that she had never seen "any black man deal with the white world

Poitier accompanied his friend and fellow actor Harry Belafonte on a mission to deliver money and moral support to civil rights workers in Mississippi. Poitier maintained that the "Ku Klux Klan tried everything except gunplay to wreck our little caravan."

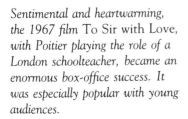

Sentimental and heartwarming, the 1967 film To Sir with Love, *with Poitier playing the role of a London schoolteacher, became an enormous box-office success. It was especially popular with young audiences.*

with his kind of self-assurance and strength." Her description of the man she loved could just as easily have fitted the characters he portrayed in *To Sir with Love, Guess Who's Coming to Dinner?,* and *In the Heat of the Night.*

In *To Sir with Love,* a low-budget English production based on the E. R. Braithwaite novel of the same name, Poitier plays an idealistic teacher working with tough, rebellious students in a school in London. It was a reversal of the role he had played 12 years earlier in *Blackboard Jungle,* in which he had been a student. The producers did not believe that the film would appeal to American audiences and delayed its release for a year. To nearly everyone's surprise, the film was a huge success. Part of the film's popularity was probably due to its heartwarming story, its catchy

musical score, and its appeal to young people. A 1967 Gallup Poll revealed an even more important reason for the film's success: Poitier was the most popular star in motion pictures that year. The public apparently would flock to see Poitier in any film.

Poitier appeared next in *Guess Who's Coming to Dinner?*, a story about an interracial marriage engagement. In this film, he had the opportunity to work with Spencer Tracy and Katharine Hepburn under the direction once again of Stanley Kramer. This was the last film appearance of Spencer Tracy, who was gravely ill and would die 10 days after the shooting was completed. Poitier was intimidated by the great actor. During some of the scenes, he found it impossible to act in Tracy's presence and was forced to speak his lines to a empty chair instead of the actor.

The 1967 film Guess Who's Coming to Dinner? *paired Poitier with legendary screen stars Spencer Tracy and Katharine Hepburn (right). It was the second of two films that Poitier made that year to be nominated for an Academy Award for Best Picture; the other film was* In the Heat of the Night.

Controversy surrounded *Guess Who's Coming to Dinner?* Cast as the distinguished surgeon John Prentice, Poitier was never allowed to give his intended bride more than an affectionate hug. To black critics, many of whom were strongly influenced by the radical black power movement then taking place, the film seemed to be saying that only the most accomplished of black men were worthy of marrying a white woman. The subdued nature of the relationship between the black doctor and his fiancée was also criticized. The novelist James Baldwin wryly summed up these feelings, saying he believed that "*Guess Who's Coming to Dinner?* may prove, in some bizarre way, to be a milestone, because it is really quite impossible to go any further in that particular direction. The next time, the kissing will have to start."

In describing Poitier's plight in such movies, film critic Hollis Alpert wrote that unlike Gary Cooper, one of the leading white actors in the 1940s and 1950s, "Poitier isn't allowed to get the girl (or even *a* girl) in the end, and all the handsome masculinity he represents must wait for the day when mores and attitudes change sufficiently to allow him to respond to love signals sent his way by white heroines who aren't particularly concerned about color barriers." However, Poitier was determined to play more romantic parts, and that meant kissing the woman he loved. He said, "From now on the pattern, according to my scheme, is that I will continue to be a hero. But I won't be a neuter."

Guess Who's Coming to Dinner? also stirred up much controversy in the South, where white racists picketed outside the movie houses that were showing the film to protest its depiction of an engagement of a black man and a white woman. But most Americans believed the film made a brave and valuable attempt to confront some of the country's most troubling racial issues. Overall, Poitier was extremely happy with the film.

"As a supporter of the civil rights struggle," Poitier said, "I found myself participating most frequently by making appearances on behalf of those on the firing line." He also supported voter registration drives in the South like the one shown here.

Happy or not, Poitier was caught in the middle of the maelstrom that surrounded the film. He was repeatedly asked by black critics why showing an interracial love affair in a film was only acceptable if the black man had a list of achievements "as long as your arm." The criticisms of the roles he played was deeply frustrating to Poitier, who throughout his career had pushed hard to change the image of blacks in film.

Poitier recuperated from the turmoil surrounding *Guess Who's Coming to Dinner?* by taking his four daughters on a tour of the United States. After moving out of the family house, he had grown apart from his children, and he longed to recapture the closeness of his early days as a parent. In early 1967, rumors had been flying that he and Diahann Carroll were at last going to be married, but instead they soon split up. He subsequently felt particularly lonely and vulnerable. Bachelor life did not suit him, especially because he had grown up in a large family and was happiest in the company of relatives and friends. He returned from his tour of the United States feeling renewed and ready to begin work on his next film.

In the Heat of the Night starred Poitier as the Philadelphia police detective Virgil Tibbs and Rod Steiger as Bill Gillespie, a redneck sheriff in a small, racist southern town, where Tibbs is arrested as a suspect in the murder of a local businessman. When Gillespie discovers that Tibbs is a highly respected detective and is clearly innocent, he swallows his pride and asks for Tibbs's help in solving the murder.

The relationship that develops between Tibbs and Gillespie is the center of this minor masterpiece, for which Steiger won the Academy Award in 1967. Steiger attributed much of his success in the part to Poitier, and Poitier, in turn, attributed his success to Steiger. Nearly unanimous critical praise greeted Poitier's performance as a black detective who is forced to confront his own prejudices. The film won an Academy Award for Best Picture and was a box office hit, which was personally gratifying to Poitier, who felt vindicated after the controversy surrounding *Guess Who's Coming to Dinner?*

After making *In the Heat of the Night*, Poitier returned to Broadway for his debut as a director in *Carry Me Back to Morningside Heights*, a play by Robert Alan Aurthur, the author of *A Man Is Ten Feet Tall*. Despite a superb cast, the play lasted for only seven performances. Poitier admitted that his inexperienced directing was partially responsible for the play's early demise. Clive Barnes of the *New York Times* agreed, writing in his review of the play, "The kindest thing I could do to the play's director, Sidney Poitier, would be to avoid mention of his name." The experience did not discourage Poitier from wanting to do more directing in the future.

Poitier immortalizes his name in Hollywood in front of Grauman's Chinese Theater.

Along with directing, Poitier was also beginning to generate his own film projects. In 1968, he starred in a film called *For Love of Ivy*. The script, which was written by Robert Alan Aurthur, was based on an idea developed by Poitier, and he also arranged the financing for the film. Playing opposite actress Abbey Lincoln, Poitier appeared in his first love scene on the screen, marking another milestone for a black actor. The film dealt with the problems facing a young black woman struggling to find both a career and a romance. "There are millions of black girls in this country and almost never do they see themselves reflected on television, in movies or the theater," said Poitier, who wanted movies to provide convincing role models for young black women such as his own daughters.

Following the making of *For Love of Ivy*, Poitier announced that he intended to develop his own film projects in the future and gain financing through his own production company. "Art has the responsibility to teach, to illuminate, to provoke," he said in an interview at the time. He wanted to make sure his films would fulfill these requirements. For the first time in his career, Poitier would have artistic and economic freedom.

Ironically, this new freedom came at a time when the public was rushing to see a new film genre, which came to be called the black exploitation movie. In these films, the angry black hero, often depicted as a pimp or gangster, is shown revenging himself upon opponents such as double-crossing drug dealers and Mafia gunmen. The black exploitation movies were noisy and violent and filled with a charged-up hatred of the white establishment. During this period, Poitier's quieter presence on the screen and his nonconfrontational style fell into disfavor. His film career suddenly slipped, as he says, "into a kind of twilight zone." ◖◗

8

HIS
OWN BOSS

IT IS MONEY and Poitier's ability to make it, both for himself and others, that give him the power and leverage he commands in Hollywood today," wrote a film critic in 1977, describing Poitier's return to the screen at the age of 50, after a period of declining popularity in the early 1970s. His box office appeal had waned as the civil rights movement lost much of its former impetus and the attention of many frustrated and angry blacks was claimed by *Shaft*, *Superfly*, *Cotton Comes to Harlem*, and other black exploitation films.

Poitier had no interest in making exploitation films, no matter how profitable they were. "My understanding of the film business told me that the [white] producers who were making black exploitation films were not interested in much beyond the buck," he said. "Past the point where that buck stopped, there wasn't a genuine interest in the black audience."

During the 1960s and early 1970s, Poitier's commitment to crossover films (films that appeal to black and white audiences) continued to be attacked by the more radical elements of the black community. "I didn't particularly relish criticism of my work as 'too white,' " Poitier said of the movies he made

---

Poitier said of his success, "It pleased me greatly to be thought of . . . as someone who had done very well as an actor, for whom hard work had paid off."

during this period. "I got a lot of bad vibes from some of my actor friends." His commitment to crossover films was based not only on his personal artistic preferences but also on sound business logic. Low-budget exploitation films did not have to draw a huge number of viewers to be profitable. However, Poitier's more expensive films had to appeal to both white and black audiences in order to make any money.

Although black exploitation films were made by white Hollywood producers, they provided employment for many black actors and directors. Few of these individuals were willing to acknowledge Poitier's role in opening up more opportunities for black performers. He felt somewhat embittered that younger black actors refused to give him the credit he thought he deserved. Consequently, he was especially touched by a gesture made by Jim Brown, the former star football player turned actor, who walked over to him on an airplane flight they were sharing and said, "A lot of things are happening now and a lot of us are working. I just thought I'd stroll up here and say 'thank you' for the contribution you've made to us all having a little piece."

Poitier's sense of isolation from other black actors stemmed in part from the fact that the roles he was now remembered for—distinguished, middle-class professionals—were ones that many blacks felt were the creations of white producers and writers who had no real understanding of black culture. Having battled against Hollywood's false images of blacks throughout his career, Poitier well understood the frustration that other black performers were feeling. But about his own work, he wrote, "I knew that however inadequate my step appeared, it was important that we make it. From one step would come another step, however overdue, and every new step would bring us closer."

Once Poitier decided to become his own boss and develop his own film projects, he was free to create a new screen image for himself. In 1969, he made *The Lost Man*, in which he plays a militant black political activist who becomes a hunted criminal after organizing a major robbery. The film broke new ground for Poitier because his character has an affair with a white social worker that culminates in a love scene. Although the film was a box office failure, it presented Poitier in a harder-edged role than the saintly type of characters he had played so often in the past.

After *The Lost Man* was completed, Poitier and two other screen stars, Paul Newman and Barbra Streisand, agreed to form their own film production outfit, First Artists Production Company. The company was designed to give each of the performers artistic and financial control over their films. Al-

Audiences generally expect a major star to play a certain type of role. Consequently, the movie-going public did not take to Poitier's performance as a black militant in the 1969 film The Lost Man.

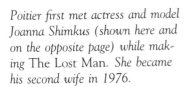
Poitier first met actress and model Joanna Shimkus (shown here and on the opposite page) while making The Lost Man. *She became his second wife in 1976.*

though Poitier continued to appear in films made by other Hollywood studios, the new arrangement allowed him to pursue his own projects as well.

In 1970, Poitier decided that he needed time away from the fast pace of Hollywood life. He moved to the Bahamas and worked on developing new ideas for films. However, he kept a home in Beverly Hills, California, to which he returned whenever he was shooting a film.

The serenity of a newly built home in Nassau seemed to be exactly what Poitier needed. Living with him was his new love interest, the actress and model Joanna Shimkus, whom he had met while working on *The Lost Man.* The film's producers had invited the blond model to audition for a part in the movie after she had appeared on the cover of *Vogue* magazine. Poitier formed an instant liking for Shimkus when she refused to take a screen test. She believed that the producers should be able to judge her talent from her appearances in a few other minor films. Of a rebellious nature himself, Poitier said he liked Shimkus's "mischievous disrespect for the rules of the picture business," and once again he found himself

falling in love with a woman whom he had first seen on a magazine cover.

Before filming of *The Lost Man* even began, Poitier started a long-distance courtship of Shimkus, sending flowers to her at her home in Paris. The romance blossomed on the set, and Shimkus moved to the Bahamas with Poitier when he decided to establish his base of operations in Nassau in 1970.

While living in Nassau, Poitier made many trips to the United States and other places on business. In the relatively peaceful political climate of the Bahamas, which was enjoying black majority rule after having recently gained independence from Great Britain, Poitier found a welcome respite from the racial unrest in the United States. He also enjoyed a period of tranquility in his personal life. Joanna Shimkus had a calming effect on him, and he was overjoyed about the birth of their daughters, Anika and Sidnee, in the early 1970s.

Few of the films that Poitier made between 1970 and 1974 were critical successes, and none were box office bonanzas. In 1970, he starred in *They Call Me Mr. Tibbs*, portraying the detective he had made fa-

Poitier with actor Harry Belafonte (left) and actress Ruby Dee (right) in the 1972 film Buck and the Preacher. Poitier and Belafonte both produced the film, which also marked Poitier's directorial debut.

mous in *In the Heat of the Night*. The film received poor reviews, and its sequel, *The Organization*, did only marginally better. In 1971, *Brother John* presented Poitier in the role of a man with strange powers who visits an Alabama town that is experiencing a strike by black workers against the local factory.

Poitier's best film of the period was *Buck and the Preacher*, which he coproduced and in which he costarred with Harry Belafonte. "We wanted black people to see the film and be proud of themselves, be proud of their history," Poitier said about the film, which portrays a group of former slaves who leave Louisiana in the 1880s to homestead in the West. "As artists we wanted to make a loving comment about the people we represent."

Released in 1972, *Buck and the Preacher* was, in some ways, a film before its time. It was more akin in spirit to *Roots*, Alex Haley's Pulitzer Prize-winning book about his search for stories about his ancestors, than it was to the black exploitation films of the early 1970s, with which it had to compete at the box office. Although it was an accomplished film, it was not a money-maker.

Buck and the Preacher was the first film to be directed by Poitier. He had not been planning to make his film directing debut for a few more years, but when the initial work of the person hired to direct the movie proved to be disappointing, Belafonte talked Poitier into taking on the job so that the distributor would not cancel the project. Recalling the terror he felt on his first day in the director's chair, Poitier said, "After three or four takes of that first scene, a calm came over me. . . . And I, as green as I was, had a touch for this new craft I had been courting from a distance for many many years." Although it was difficult to direct and act in the same film, Poitier found directing to be rewarding because it allowed him to exert a lot of control over the finished product.

In 1973, Poitier produced, directed, and played the lead in *A Warm December*, a love story about a widowed American doctor who travels to London with his young daughter and falls in love with an African princess. The first film that Poitier made under his arrangement with First Artists, *A Warm December* was panned by the critics and lost a lot of money.

By the mid-1970s, the black exploitation film craze had begun to subside. Poitier had proven to himself and to the Hollywood establishment that a rich and influential independent black producer could survive hostile marketplace conditions. Even after five years of declining box office ratings, he still had the clout to put together the financial package that was necessary to make an expensive Hollywood movie.

Years of introspection and experimenting with film stories had convinced Poitier that he wanted to make movies such as *Uptown Saturday Night* which celebrate the joy of life. "The success of *Uptown Saturday Night*," he wrote about the high-spirited 1975 comedy he directed and acted in with Bill Cosby, Harry Belafonte, and Richard Pryor, "told me that black people wanted to laugh at themselves and have fun. They were weary of being represented on the local screen by pimps, hustlers, prostitutes, private detectives, violence, macho men and dirty words." *Uptown Saturday Night* was a huge financial success, and it convinced the heads of the film industry that Poitier was still a star.

In 1975, Poitier appeared with Michael Caine in a thriller called *The Wilby Conspiracy*. Shot in Kenya, the film starred Poitier as a South African revolutionary. His next film, *Let's Do It Again*, a sequel to *Uptown Saturday Night*, starred Poitier and Cosby as two friends involved in hilarious shenanigans as they try to outwit two mobsters. *Let's Do It Again* was even more successful than its predecessor and confirmed to Poitier that he was right that audiences wanted to see entertaining comedy adventures. Film industry analysts called the film a crossover success because it was immensely popular with both black and white audiences.

After the success of *Uptown Saturday Night* and *Let's Do It Again*, the 48-year-old Poitier slowed down. He no longer felt that he had to prove he could survive in Hollywood, and he wanted to spend more time with his family. In 1976, he married Joanna Shimkus in a quiet ceremony in their Beverly Hills home. Harry Belafonte was the best man, and his wife, Julie, acted as bridesmaid.

In 1977, Poitier teamed again with Bill Cosby in *A Piece of the Action*, which continued the successful formula of *Uptown Saturday Night* and *Let's Do It*

Again. He then took two years off from his film career to write his autobiography.

"My years had been so full, I wanted to itemize them while I was still lucid," said Poitier about his book, *This Life,* which was published in 1980. "More important was that people, even those close to me, tend to relate to the image of me projected in my films." He wanted to present a more accurate view of the restless, introspective, often troubled man who has portrayed so many cool, controlled characters on the screen.

Writing his autobiography gave Poitier the opportunity to look back on his life and his career and to make his plans for the future. He intended to continue focusing his producing and directing efforts on upbeat, funny movies. In 1980, he said that he

Poitier and entertainer Bill Cosby (left) star in the 1975 film Let's Do It Again. *A sequel to* Uptown Saturday Night, *this rollicking comedy firmly established Poitier as a Hollywood producer and director and spurred yet another sequel,* A Piece of the Action.

According to Poitier, he turned to filmmaking when he "noticed a dangerous disregard of the hopes and aspirations of black people" by other filmmakers.

did not plan to do any more acting until a "piece of material comes along that compliments my years." At the time, few people thought he was serious, but he was just recognizing the fact that he was getting older and good roles for black actors his age are not plentiful.

Because of Poitier's absence from the screen from 1977 to 1987, a whole new generation of moviegoers has not experienced Poitier's special charisma as an actor. His three most recent directorial efforts, *Stir Crazy*, *Hanky Panky*, and *Fast Forward*, were very successful at the box office, but as the director, he stayed out of the public eye. *Fast Forward*, released in 1985, is a story about a group of dancers from the Midwest who come to New York to participate in a dance competition. It is a story about young and talented people struggling to survive by using their wits, working hard, and remaining true to their dreams in a corrupting and corrupted world. Naturally, it is a story that appeals to Poitier because it mirrors the beginning of his own career.

In 1987, the 60-year-old Poitier returned to the screen to play an FBI agent in the film *Little Nikita*. He is also scheduled to appear in *In the Hall of the Mountain King* and *Hard Knox*. Once again, he is finding roles that challenge him.

Summing up the effect that he has had on the film industry and American society, Poitier said, "I think my life, on balance, has been a positive one. I think I have left some healthy dents in this old world." As a person who has constantly broken new ground and overturned old barriers, it appears certain that Poitier will leave many more marks on the world before his long journey is completed. ❧

APPENDIX

——— ❧ ———

THE FILMS OF
SIDNEY POITIER

1950   *No Way Out*
1951   *Red Ball Express*
1952   *Cry, the Beloved Country*
1954   *Go, Man, Go!*
1955   *Blackboard Jungle*
1956   *Goodbye, My Lady*
1957   *Band of Angels; Something of Value; Edge of the City*
1958   *The Defiant Ones; The Mark of the Hawk; Virgin Island*
1959   *Porgy and Bess*
1960   *All the Young Men*
1961   *A Raisin in the Sun; Paris Blues*
1962   *Pressure Point*
1963   *Lilies of the Field*
1964   *The Long Ships*
1965   *The Bedford Incident; The Slender Thread; The Greatest Story Ever Told; A Patch of Blue*
1966   *Duel at Diablo*
1967   *To Sir with Love; In the Heat of the Night; Guess Who's Coming to Dinner*
1968   *For Love of Ivy*
1969   *The Lost Man*
1970   *They Call Me Mister Tibbs*
1971   *The Organization; Brother John*
1972   *Buck and the Preacher*
1973   *A Warm December*
1974   *Uptown Saturday Night*
1975   *The Wilby Conspiracy; Let's Do It Again*
1977   *A Piece of the Action*
1980   *Stir Crazy*
1982   *Hanky Panky*
1985   *Fast Forward*
1987   *Little Nikita*

CHRONOLOGY

Feb. 20, 1927	Born Sidney Poitier in Miami, Florida
1937	Moves from Cat Island in the Bahamas to Nassau, the Bahamas
1943	Moves to Miami and then to New York City
Nov. 1943	Joins the army
Dec. 1944	Released from the army; returns to New York City
1946	Begins drama classes with the American Negro Theatre; performs in *Lysistrata*
1946–1949	Tours with *Anna Lucasta*
1950	Appears in first feature film, *No Way Out*
1951	Appears in *Cry The Beloved Country*, filmed in South Africa
1952	Marries Juanita Hardy; first daughter, Beverly, born
1954	Second daughter, Pamela, born; Poitier asked to take "loyalty oath" by Hollywood producers
1955	Appears in *Blackboard Jungle*
1957	Appears in television production of *A Man Is Ten Feet Tall*; moves to Mount Vernon, New York, with family; third daughter, Sherri, born
1959	Appears in *Porgy and Bess* and in Broadway and film versions of *A Raisin in the Sun*
1961	Fourth daughter, Gina, born
1963	Appears in *Lilies of the Field*; separates from wife, Juanita
April 1964	Receives Academy Award for Best Actor for *Lilies of the Field*
1967	Appears in *To Sir with Love, Guess Who's Coming to Dinner?*, and *In the Heat of the Night*; Gallup poll declares Poitier most popular actor
1969	Forms the First Artists' Production Company with Paul Newman and Barbra Streisand; appears in *The Last Man* with Joanna Shimkus
1972	Directs and appears in *Buck and the Preacher*; fifth daughter, Anika, born
1973	Sixth daughter, Sidnee, born
1975	Directs and appears in *Uptown Saturday Night*
1976	Directs and appears in *Let's Do It Again*; marries Joanna Shimkus
1980	Publishes autobiography, *This Life*
1985	Directs *Fast Forward*
1987	Resumes acting career

FURTHER READING

Hoffman, William. *Sidney*. Secaucus, NJ: Lyle Stuart, 1971.

Keyser, Lester J. *The Cinema of Sidney Poitier*. New York: Barnes, 1980.

Murray, James P. *To Find an Image: Black Films from Uncle Tom to Superfly*. Boston: Bobbs-Merrill, 1973.

Null, Gary. *Black Hollywood: The Black Performers in Motion Pictures*. Secaucus, NJ: Citadel, 1975.

Poitier, Sidney. *This Life*. New York: Ballantine/Knopf, 1980.

INDEX

PICTURE CREDITS

Courtesy of The Academy of Motion Picture Arts and Sciences and Columbia Pictures: p. 88; Courtesy of The Academy of Motion Picture Arts and Sciences and Metro-Goldwyn-Mayer Pictures: p. 66; Courtesy of The Academy of Motion Picture Arts and Sciences and Paramount Studios: p. 83; Courtesy of The Academy of Motion Picture Arts and Sciences and Universal Studios: pp. 97, 99; AP/Wide World Photos: pp. 57, 78, 94; Bahamas News Bureau: pp. 18, 20, 22, 24; *Films of Sidney Poitier* by Alvin H. Marill, 1978, Citadel Press: pp. 60, 68, 92, 98; *Films of Sidney Poitier* by Alvin H. Marill, 1978, Citadel Press/The Oscar statuette is a trademark and appears courtesy of The Academy of Motion Picture Arts and Sciences: p. 10; The Museum of Modern Art/Film Stills Archive: p. 26; The Museum of Modern Art/Film Stills Archive and Columbia Pictures: pp. 86–87, 100, 104; The Museum of Modern Art/Film Stills Archive and 20th Century Fox: p. 13; The Museum of Modern Art/Film Stills Archive and United Artists: p. 70; The Museum of Modern Art/Film Stills Archive and Warner Brothers, Inc.: pp. 44–45, 103; Reuters/Bettmann Newsphotos: p. 50; The Schomburg Center for Research in Black Culture, Astor, Lenox and Tilden Foundations: pp. 16, 28, 33, 38, 40, 46, 49, 65, 76, 90; The Springer/Bettmann Film Archive and Columbia Pictures: p. 77; The Springer/Bettmann Film Archive and London Films: p. 55; The Springer/Bettmann Film Archive and Metro-Goldwyn-Mayer Pictures: pp. 80, 84; The Springer/Bettmann Film Archive/United Artists Studios/ Rainbow Productions: p. 12; UPI/Bettmann Newsphotos: pp. 15, 35, 36, 37, 53, 63, 72, 75, 79, 85.

CAROL BERGMAN, a media consultant and critic, is on the faculty of The New School for Social Research in New York City. She writes a regular column for *Family Circle* magazine and has contributed articles to many other publications, including *Cineaster, Ms.,* and the *New York Times.* She is also the author of *Mae West* in the Chelsea House series "American Women of Achievement."

NATHAN IRVIN HUGGINS is W.E.B. Du Bois Professor of History and Director of the W.E.B. Du Bois Institute for Afro-American Research at Harvard University. He previously taught at Columbia University. Professor Huggins is the author of numerous books, including *Black Odyssey: The Afro-American Ordeal in Slavery, The Harlem Renaissance,* and *Slave and Citizen: The Life of Frederick Douglass.*